THE AUTHORITY ADVISOR

IF YOUR PROSPECTS CAN'T FIND YOU ONLINE, THEN YOU DON'T EXIST...

Joe Simonds

ISBN: 1500387010
ISBN 13: 9781500387013
Library of Congress Control Number: 2014912289
CreateSpace Independent Publishing Platform
North Charleston, South Carolina

For my wife, Loren, who took the brunt of the late-night work with our newborn so that I could write this book within my goal of 30 days or less.

For Luke, my brother and loyal business partner.

For Dan the Man, my daily inspiration to never give up or complain about anything beyond my control.

For my parents, for deciding to keep me after all of the trouble that I gave them as a kid.

Finally, for my two little daughters, Shauna and Savannah, who put a smile on my face every morning.

CONTENTS

PREFACE

THE AUTHORITY REVOLUTION

Do you like music? More specifically, do you love music like I do?

As a young boy growing up in the '80s, I was really into music, and I accumulated a massive collection of cassette tapes in a short span of time. This was mostly thanks to Columbia House getting me hooked on 12 cassettes for pennies each at a young age (of course, they made their money up on the back end when they charged me full retail price after my initial order). Almost all of my yard work money went to buying new music, as I just couldn't get enough of it.

I can still vividly recall the following events, all occurring in a very short amount of time, that revolutionized how we purchased, listened to, and consumed music:

- I still remember the Christmas when I received my first dual cassette "boom box," where I could play a cassette tape on one side and record it simultaneously on the other side. You would have thought that I had died and gone to music heaven! To find the right brand and version, my mother and I went to Radio Shack to compare the different boom boxes. After I told her the precise one I wanted, she drove back at a later date to pick it up and pay for it. (Seems archaic to have to go into a store as the only option, doesn't it? And this was not that long ago...

in the mid-1980s.) Did I mention that this big, heavy, clunky boom box cost over $350?

- Just a few short years later, CDs started to make their way into stores and into daily conversations with other music lovers. However, most music lovers refused to believe that cassette tapes would ever go away.
- Regardless of CDs, I still recall the excitement of getting my first bright-yellow Sony Walkman with a single cassette deck and yellow ear buds.
- However, CDs quickly went mainstream as people realized how much more efficient they were to use (no more rewinding or having to worry about the cassette tape going bad), and they gradually gained a larger section at the local record store, Specs, in my hometown.
- As CD prices went down, cassette tapes drastically dropped their prices at a feeble attempt to delay the inevitable.
- Before you knew it, cassette tapes were on their way to becoming extinct.
- The introduction of the Sony CD Walkman made it possible to listen to CDs on the go without a bulky "boom box," and my Sony "cassette" Walkman hit Goodwill shelves, replaced by my new Sony CD Walkman.
- Then, Columbia Music started sending me new offers on CDs that I simply couldn't pass up, and my collection of CDs began its infancy.
- Just a decade later, in 2001, Apple released the first iPod, with which Steve Jobs famously gave us "1,000 songs in your pocket;" this started to put pressure on CD sales.
- Just a year later, in 2002, the second-generation iPod held upward of 4,000 songs.
- Between 1999 and 2001, Napster hit the scene and sped up music "going digital" even more.
- In April of 2003, Apple introduced 99-cent songs in their iTunes Music Store.

- By September of 2003, Apple sold over 10 million songs and approached 2 million total iPods sold.
- The rest is music history, as many of today's new computers, vehicles, and music machines don't even have a place to insert a CD. Our music is stored digitally via phones, iTunes, or other digital accounts.
- And this entire multi-extinction music revolution from cassettes, to CDs, to digital occurred in less than 25 years.
- Today, my CDs have been burned to my iTunes (thus my iPhone, iPad, and iMac), and my entire collection is buried somewhere in a box in the attic.
- My latest purchase was an Apple TV that I ordered online at www.applestore.com after going to a few websites and reading reviews, even watching a video on how it works. It arrived just a few days after ordering and paying for it online (without speaking to anyone or driving anywhere to touch and feel it). This device lets me play my 10,000-plus songs anywhere I want to, including through any TV or computer, and even surround sound systems pretty much anywhere in the world. And it is small enough to put in my coat pocket.
- Oh, by the way, did I mention that I made the purchase on my laptop while on a babymoon with my wife at the top of a private mountain villa in St. Lucia?
- Boy, things sure have changed a lot in terms of access to information and ease of buying in just 20 years.

Another amazing story that would have sounded completely implausible just a decade ago occurred last year when my wife and I found out that we were going to move from Houston, Texas to Atlanta, Georgia.

My wife was in her final year of residency at medical school in Houston. She had zero vacation days left, as she burned through them all to have our first child, when we received the exciting news that my wife was accepted to join an incredible private practice in Atlanta.

The only problem was that my wife literally couldn't get a single day off to fly to Atlanta to check out homes for us to live in. We were scheduled to move in just six months, and I couldn't take off on the weekends, as we had no family or help in Houston to watch our one-year-old while my wife worked (every single weekend).

So, what did we do?

One weekend, we spent some time on Zillow.com and started looking at houses around the area near her office. Although we had both lived in Atlanta many years earlier, neither of us ever ventured up to the suburban area where her new office was. After an hour or two of searching, we narrowed it down to two houses we liked. Since we knew that we were going to move into a house sight unseen (at least not in the flesh), we decided to rent with the option to buy if we liked the house.

We skipped hiring a real estate agent completely and simply contacted the owner directly from Zillow to ask a few questions.

My only request was that the owner use her iPhone to take a virtual video tour of the house, upload it to YouTube, and send the link over for us to view when she was done. This was to ensure that we were seeing the most updated version of the home, as some people have been known to post older pictures of their homes on the web.

By that evening, we had the video, and we absolutely loved everything we saw. Did I mention this was all from the comfort of our own townhouse in downtown Houston?

The next day, we put our deposit down via an online transfer, and a few months later we moved from Houston to Atlanta, excited to see our new house in person for the first time. You gotta love technology!

These are just two (of many) of my personal stories about how technology has changed the way society consumes and digests everyday products and services in our lives. Transparency and access to almost unlimited information have certainly changed how products and services are bought and sold today.

What is clear is that anytime a new technology enables us to receive things faster (to save time) or cheaper and more efficiently (to save money), it is only a matter of time before the old-school ways that refuse to adapt gradually become obsolete.

More importantly, those who adapt, embrace, and capitalize on the changes will achieve ultimate authority in their communities and industries.

And that is really what this book is about... *adaptation* and *authority*. **Adaptation** in terms of how your clients want to be sold, how they want to get information, and the ideal kind of relationship today's consumers want to have with you; and **authority** to be the expert in your area who is providing your ideal prospects and clients with information and education, so that when they are ready to buy, you are at the top of their minds as the go-to authority and expert. The authority to be the #1 recommended expert in your area. The authority to gain and maintain your ideal prospects' and clients' trust, to give openly without fear of competitors, and to gain complete control of your sales pipeline.

This book is also about changing your marketing strategy. The average American is bombarded with over 3,000 unique marketing messages every single day. Later in the book, I refer to this as "interruption marketing," as it is literally trying to interrupt what we are doing, vying for our attention.

Unfortunately, interruption marketing does not work like it used to, which is why many of the "old ways" of marketing are losing their effect at a rapid rate. But the great news is that this book reveals how to grab your ideal prospects' attention without interrupting them, and just as important, how to keep their attention and get your prospects to take action.

The Financial Services Industry

The information, tactics, and theories presented in this book really apply to any and all industries, small business owners, entrepreneurs, and proprietors. However, I have written this book with a story about a financial advisor and his wild journey of adaptation in this new world. And the reason that I picked a financial advisor is because it is the industry that I have served for the past 12 years, I know it well, and I want to see it thrive going forward.

For those of you who are not financial advisors, simply substitute your profession for "financial advisor," and you will certainly see that we are all faced with the same changes, regardless of your business, your goals, or your clients.

On the financial advisor front in particular, not many other people have had the courage to stick their heads up and risk becoming unpopular by telling hundreds of thousands of financial professionals that they might soon be extinct. But the writing is on the wall, and any time I share my beliefs with people in our industry, I usually get a nod of agreement followed by, "Yep, but who is going to warn and educate the financial professionals before it becomes too late?"

For the record, I am writing this book and giving this stern warning not to make money on book sales, not to create friends, and not to create enemies, but rather to give you the truth on what I believe is happening right in front of our eyes. I care about this industry, as it has provided for my family and me for the last 12 years, and I will do anything in my power to make sure that this industry continues to excel, instead of floundering like cassette tapes did in the '90s.

And if I can help you see the warning signs and avoid extinction as a financial professional or any other professional or entrepreneur, then my job here with this book is complete, and the process is worth every minute it took me to write this.

The Three Main Issues Today for Financial Professionals

This book is the full story about the struggles, the near-divorce, the near-sale of his company, the "I'm about to throw in the towel," and finally, the ultimate success and transformation of financial advisor Steve Kennedy in Winter Park, Florida.

In this story, you will pick up on the following three problems that I am willing to bet most of you have experienced, or will experience soon, in your very own practice.

- The old ways of marketing, like seminars, radio, and direct mail, are becoming less reliable and effective with each year that goes by. In many parts of the country, these "tried and true" marketing tactics are not only losing steam; in some cases, they are dying a slow death. The costs of marketing, branding, and advertising continue to increase, while the ROI (Return on Investment) goes down each year. At some point, this bubble will pop.

- Your baby boomer and senior clients are online today, not only looking up everything from retirement topics to pictures of their grandkids, but also buying big-ticket items online... including financial plans, TVs, new cars, annuities, life insurance, second homes, and so on. Today's boomers and retirees are receiving (and demanding) their information on everything online, from how they look up the best plumber, to finding the cheapest airline tickets, to acquiring financial information. And boy, does it look different than it did just five to seven years ago! And if they can't get their information and education in the desired form, they quickly move on to another company or person who can give it to them on their terms. To make matters worse, most of you have lost at least one client to an online advisor, whether you know it or not. In the near future, if your clients can't find you and your business online, then it doesn't exist.
- If you are like many financial professionals, you lack full control of your sales funnel and rely either partially or fully on third-party groups to create your new leads and prospects. Of course, you would prefer to control your entire sales funnel, automate your practice and have ideal prospects find you online, and be able to work more from home so that you could live the lifestyle you have always dreamed of, one full of traveling, spending more time with your family, donating to charity, and helping more people around you. But it just hasn't worked out that way for most of you... yet.

If any of this sounds remotely familiar, it should, as I have found that most financial professionals today struggle with anywhere from one to all three of these problems.

Let's face it, the world is always changing around us. But with the rise of the Internet and new technologies that continue to eliminate weak links (including weak salespeople and weak distribution lines), marketing in the financial services industry, and all industries for that matter, is literally being turned on its head right now.

Before I give you some examples in our financial services world, let's talk about just how much has changed in terms of marketing, messaging, and information sharing since 2004.

Do you recall reading the newspaper not long ago to get your news on everything from current events, sports, the community, and so on? Do you still read the morning paper? Some of you do, but I am willing to bet the majority of you get your daily information from some phone app or the Internet.

Personally, I still have the morning paper delivered to my house. But 9 out of 10 days, it never even leaves the plastic wrapper before hitting the trash can. I would be willing to bet that my three-year-old daughter gets more use out of our paper for her art projects than I do actually getting new information. So, if you are anything like most Americans, you are relying on the morning paper for your information less and less each year, or in many cases, you don't read the paper any more at all.

And if you do, it is probably only to glance at headlines to see if there was anything that you somehow overlooked online. And if you think about it, with the ability to get up-to-date information from a device that is in most of our hands or pockets for 90 percent of our waking day, why would we want to read about news or information that is already a day old?

"What Is a Phone Book?" My Daughter Asked

Do you recall pulling out the phone book to look up a company's information?

Do you still do that today, or do you pull out the smartphone from your pocket, purse, or jacket (or it is already in the grip of your hand, like most of us) and just do a quick search?

You don't have to answer, because I already know the answer. In fact, just this week as I was writing this, I went out to bring our trash can back in from the street around 6 o'clock in the evening on trash day. On my way to the edge of the street, I noticed that a new Yellow Pages phone book was in a plastic wrapper in the middle of the driveway. I quickly picked it up, admired it (as it might be the last year I receive one), and then threw it in the empty trash bin before wheeling it back down toward the house.

And guess what? I bet 9 out of 10 of my neighbors did the same thing. Why let something like that take up space when it is already out of date compared to the Internet?

A little over a year ago, I was in the market to buy a new vehicle. The great news was that I knew I wanted a 2014 Chevrolet Tahoe. I wasn't sure what kind of package and accessories I wanted, but I knew the kind of vehicle I wanted.

So, instead of hopping in my car and spending an entire weekend going around from dealership to dealership, having to deal with a dreaded car salesperson, having to hear the dog and pony show over and over again, test-driving all of the different vehicles, and then starting the negotiations to see which dealer could possibly give me the best deal, I decided to hit the Internet first.

My first Google search was for Chevy dealerships in Houston. I was shocked to see that there were at least 12 of them in and around the Houston area! I narrowed it down to the top three near my zip code and then went to each of their websites to see which one was the easiest to navigate and had the most information.

One of them came out as the clear winner, as the dealership had taken the time to go above and beyond with a "build your dream vehicle" option. It also had loads of pictures, videos, and even reviews of the different Tahoes.

And before you knew it, I built my custom Tahoe. I added in all of the "extras" that I wanted (I was even able to see what the custom wheels I wanted would look like on the new Tahoe), and I had the entire thing priced out at MSRP.

My next few searches were looking for this exact same model for sale on other sites to get an idea of price fluctuations, and I found what I needed in short order.

After talking it over with my wife, we agreed on a price we were willing to pay, and I made a phone call to the dealership that I liked (keep in mind that there was another dealership just as close, if not closer, to my house) to see if they would play ball.

I asked for the manager and told him exactly what I was looking for. I told him that I completed all of my research online and didn't even need to test-drive a car, and if he would agree to my price (not his or his salespeople's price), then I would drive down there today and sign the paperwork.

He agreed, I went down there and signed the paperwork, and then I drove away with a new Tahoe a week later (they didn't have the exact model on the lot). I never had to speak to a salesman, barter or negotiate, and it was an awesome experience. All because I had so much information at my fingertips.

Do you know why I went with the specific dealership that I did? It was because it was the one with the most *authority* in terms of transparent and free information online.

And even if we don't consciously realize it, we all choose companies and services every year for the very same reason, which is known as reciprocity. We were taught at a young age that when someone gives us something out of the blue or for free, we feel obligated to reciprocate and give back. Not to mention, most people love to get things for free, and they usually don't forget the people, brands, or companies that enrich their lives with free information, samples, products, or services.

Have you ever had a family member, neighbor, or coworker give you a gift out of the blue? Or perhaps it was Christmas or Hanukkah and someone gave you a gift, but you forgot to get him or her one? For some reason (called the reciprocity factor), we actually feel guilty, and all we can think about is how we can repay that person or get him or her a gift as soon as possible.

This is the same reason that I give so much of my knowledge and so many of my secrets away for free on my site, www.AdvisorInternetMarketing.com. I fully realize that people exist who have way more talent and knowledge than I about digital marketing. However, if all of their tips and content are hidden behind "pay-only" doors, most of you will never take the chance to buy it, since you haven't built any trust or any relationship with that expert.

On the other hand, if you have been receiving my free weekly sales ideas, blogs, and live hangouts, all packed full of valuable free content, by the time you are ready to "go digital," the chances are really high that you will come back to me, as we have already established trust, a relationship, and reciprocity.

Sadly, most small business owners (including financial advisors) do just the opposite, hiding all of their valuable advice and knowledge and only sharing with prospects and clients who meet them face-to-face or hire them. There is the fear that competitors might learn something, that they might even steal some of your valuable content—but I am telling you, just the opposite occurs.

In reality, prospects are magnetically attracted to you when you put your best stuff out in public and start educating people. Being truthful, helpful, and transparent can literally change your business.

Ironically, your competitors start fearing you and wondering how they can ever compete with someone who has so much great content, as they all assume that you would never put your best information and education out for everyone to see.

This precise theory applies to all industries, products, and services. And it certainly applies to financial professionals. If you can muster the courage to share openly and freely, you will begin to see the magic of reciprocity and authority for yourself.

The Information Evolution

Let's face it, the way we get information and education and the way that we buy things has changed drastically, and it will continue to evolve. And because other companies, industries, and services are enabling consumers to more easily solve their problems, get answers, and buy things, it has altered our expectations of how everything around us should be.

Can you imagine driving through a town in a hurry, needing a quick bite to eat before meeting with some prospects, and coming to realize that not a single fast-food stop has a drive-through window?

As you walk inside, ticked off, famished, and becoming later for your meeting by the minute, you ask the staff why they don't have a drive-through window, and they tell you with a straight face, "Because we believe our clients are different... they all like to come inside and order."

It could be true, but societal and national expectations have altered our perception and trained consumers to expect certain things in life.

It is these same consumer expectations that have forced many of you to finally have a website for your company. And it is likely that these expectations are part of why you bought this book– you don't want to get left behind by not adapting.

If you still aren't sure, then I suggest shutting down your website, changing your business card to provide only your company name, followed by "Look me up in the Yellow Pages," and see how things go...

The Death of the Salesman, the Birth of the Marketer

Some bad news first.

The old days of sending out a 3,000-piece mailer inviting people to a dinner seminar and getting 80 to 120 buying units to show up are over.

Have you noticed that now it takes you upward of 7,000 or even 10,000 mailing invitations to fill a smaller room today than you used in the past? Consumers have woken up to what is going on around them, and they have a new mindset on how they want to be "sold."

Not to mention, the constant barrage of negative articles about financial dinner seminars on high-authority sites like Forbes, The Wall Street Journal, and AARP aren't helping the cause either.

Unless you have unique, proven, and proprietary mailers in conjunction with a constantly updated, entertaining, and educational seminar, you don't stand a chance growing your business this way in the future.

Do you recall in the mid-2000s how cheap it was to get on a great radio station where you could practically say anything about "safe money strategies," annuity bonuses, and so on, and your phone would be ringing off the hook with interested seniors and boomers?

And have you noticed that today, the price of the same radio airtime is inflating faster than college tuition? Moreover, have you noticed that, even with your new strategic way of doing radio, the quantity and quality of your leads and prospects have come down drastically?

Unless you are lucky enough to have a full-time radio team like my friends over at the Impact Partnership who are pushing out ideas, content, co-hosts, and support on your behalf, you are going to have a tough time surviving on only radio marketing.

Likewise, do you remember the old 3x5 postcards with a powerful retirement message that you could send out in a single batch of 2,000 pieces and get 50 to 75 new solid lead cards back? How many 3x5 postcards would it take you to get 50 to 75 solid lead cards back today?

Many of the old-school mail houses are struggling to get 0.05 percent of mailers to convert into seminar attendees. The Impact Partnership, a marketing organization where I have quite a few close friends and colleagues, is one of the few anomalies to these failing seminar mailer rates, as they are somehow still converting (and even guaranteeing) at least a 0.5% response rate on all mailers. However, most FMOs (Field Marketing Organizations) can't touch this. And certainly none of the third-party marketing companies who target the financial services are seeing these kinds of results.

Let's face the facts: Seminar marketing in general is fading and will never see the kind of results it did in the past, unless you have a one-of-a-kind message and system in place. And even then, it will still be tough to rely on this as your only marketing tool.

The problem with the old way of marketing is twofold:

1) Today's consumers have become much smarter in terms of avoiding marketing tactics and sales pitches. From getting fooled so many times, to getting rubbed the wrong way by aggressive salespeople, to simply tuning out all of the advertising and loud messages around them, consumers are not falling for the same old tricks.
2) Today's consumers are also digesting information differently. The means to getting information on pretty much any topic known to man is not only the easiest it has been in the history of mankind, but it is also usually *free* and delivered instantly via a computer screen. I recall going to my dad's prized *Encyclopedia Britannica* signature collection to look things up when I was young. How many of you (or your clients) still use the ol' *Britannica* books to look up questions and information?

But Our Industry is Different... WRONG

Let's revisit the music revolution for a second.

Imagine if, back when it was finally becoming obvious that cassette tapes were going obsolete by way of the CD, the entire jazz industry said that because the majority of jazz listeners were older people, it didn't need to adapt and start moving its music to CDs.

You know, because the jazz industry was "different," it could still survive with its own section in music stores that would only offer cassette tapes. The industry assumed that because its target demographic was older, listeners probably wouldn't want the more efficient and reliable CDs.

"Heck, why even move away from the vinyl record?" yelled the jazz musician business.

Had this occurred, jazz music would have died a quick death alongside the record or cassette tape.

Doesn't that kind of thinking sound crazy, knowing what you know now? But this is exactly how foolish we sound when we say that our clients are different. That consumers who are looking for retirement and financial information and education want to get their information completely differently from how they get all the rest of their information.

Are you beginning to see how outrageous this kind of thinking is?

Do you know why no industry, niche, or business is "different" when an efficiency revolution is happening around it?

A must-read book by Jay Bear about why smart marketing is about help, not hype, titled *Youtility*, answers this question perfectly: "Because your customers' expectations are changing, whether you like it or not."

What this means is, it doesn't matter whether anyone in your industry is providing information or services digitally yet. All that matters is how your clients are getting the rest of the information in their lives… because if every other industry is doing something a certain way, our customers now expect the same from us, whether we like it or not.

Just as the entire jazz section of music would have eventually been pulled from the shelves and moved closer to extinction if the jazz industry had not taken its music to CDs (and eventually iTunes), the same will happen in your industry if you aren't taking your message, voice, and brand online.

What Will You Learn in This Book?

The great news is that this book will teach you how to become a powerful, transparent, effective, and authoritative marketer.

More importantly, it will teach you the process of extinction prevention—in particular, how to avoid being one of the inevitable old-school salespeople who will go by the wayside from refusing to adapt.

In fact, I am betting that the only financial professionals, small business owners, and entrepreneurs who survive and prosper between 2015 and 2025 will be those who understand marketing, learn transparent marketing, and learn how to effectively communicate and build relationships with their ideal clients in this new era of information and commerce.

And the only ones to truly come out stronger and better than ever before will be those entrepreneurs who realize that salespeople must be effective marketers before they ever put on their sales hats.

How Do You Like to Receive Your Information?

Let me ask you a personal question about how you prefer to get your information today versus in the past.

If you need to get information or education on a problem that you are trying to solve, which method would you use today?

a. Wait on an invitation in the mail to a free dinner seminar
b. Hope that someone will talk about the problem you are trying to solve on the TV or radio this weekend
c. Get out the Yellow Pages and start randomly calling salespeople or companies that you hope might have some answers
d. Look up the problem online immediately

I thought so.

But this isn't to say that these old methods are going away completely. For instance, let's dissect the *Encyclopedia Britannica* example. For decades, *Encyclopedia Britannica* books were the way Americans got information and learned just about anything they wanted to if they knew what letter the word started with.

However, the Internet came along and essentially made the *Encyclopedia Britannica* extinct in no time at all. On the other hand, doesn't Wikipedia mirror the exact same end goal that *Encyclopedia Britannica* had, only more efficiently and cheaper (free), while providing the user a more enjoyable experience overall?

You can bet your bottom dollar it does.

This same revolution can be found throughout our society over the past 80 years, as technology and innovation have opened up new opportunities and more efficient ways to do things. And time after time, consumers have gravitated toward and embraced anything that can speed up the solutions to their problems.

Let's take a look at a few more examples of this right here in America.

Travel agencies went extinct, only to usher in digital travel agencies like Travelocity, Priceline, and Expedia.

Ironically, railway travel went from being the only cross-country travel option in America to going almost completely extinct as more efficient and effective options became available with the airlines.

In the financial services industry, a brokerage firm opened up its doors on the complete other side of the country from Wall Street. The big-name wire houses, like Bear Stearns, Lehman Brothers, and Merrill Lynch, all laughed at this new company and didn't even consider it a competitor. That is, until this small start-up company of Wall Street rejects found a way to eliminate the expensive broker and give consumers the same stocks for a fraction of the price.

This firm's name was Charles Schwab. They truly came out of nowhere, were working out of a dilapidated building outside of San Francisco, and had little cash, yet found a way to not only compete with the big boys of Wall Street, but also steal their clients.

Today, Bear Stearns, Lehman, and Merrill have all either completely dissolved or filed bankruptcy, while Schwab continues to thrive as it continually strives to find new ways to eliminate inefficiencies and make investing simple for consumers.

Blockbuster was the staple across America for families, friends, and couples to get their movies and even video games. There was at least one Blockbuster in almost every city in America, it seemed. But within less than a few years, a no-name group with a fraction of the assets and cash as Blockbuster, called Netflix, almost entirely killed the giant. This near extinction whooping was completely due to the fact that Netflix found a more efficient way to deliver consumers the same end product.

Do you recall where you went to buy books 10 years ago? I am willing to bet most of you went to either Borders or Barnes & Noble. How many of you still get in your car and go down to the bookstore to buy books?

Given that Borders is bankrupt and Amazon is selling more books than any company in the world, my bet is most of you shop on Amazon from the comfort of your home, iPad, or any other device that you do your shopping from.

What I really want you to understand here is that the technology revolution is affecting all industries, large and small. And the moral of the story is that people today finally understand just how precious their time on Earth is.

Time is the one thing in our lives that is limited, no matter how much money we have, no matter how well we take care of our bodies, and no matter how well we avoid stress. We each have 24 hours in a day to get as much done as we can, to make the biggest impact in our lives and in the lives around us.

So any time consumers are presented with a more efficient solution to their problems that can save them time, more often than not, they will take the shorter path.

Let's be blunt about how you, as an entrepreneur, can establish relationships with new clients. If you look at it from a big-picture point of view, it is easy to see that you are usually attempting to do the following things, no matter how you market and sell yourself:

- You do your best to educate prospects on problems they have (like running out of money in retirement, if you are in the financial services industry), and on problems that they have but might not know they have (like not understanding they are losing money by not maximizing their Social Security, or not realizing the real damage of long-term care on their assets if they aren't protected)
- You also educate them on why you are the expert who can solve these problems for them
- You then try to establish credibility, trust, and rapport

These three bullets above do not change regardless of whether you are doing seminar marketing, Internet marketing, radio marketing, direct mail, referral marketing, speaking at colleges, and so on.

And the new reality in the retirement income world is that your ideal baby boomer and retiree clients are going to the Internet to get their information today.

Don't believe me?

Then how is it that the fastest growing segments of financial advisors in the industry are doing all of their marketing and sales over the Internet?

How is it that these "robo-advisors" like Wealthfront, Betterment, and Covestor are bringing in billions (with a "B") of new assets, all online, without ever meeting with clients face to face? FYI, Wealthfront, just one of many new robo-advisor groups, opened its doors back in 2008 and really didn't get momentum until years later. In less than three years, it already controlled over $1.2 billion in assets without ever meeting its clients face to face.

Want more proof? Simply call up some of your clients and tell them that you have forms for them to sign, and they can either come in and see you face to face… *or* that you could just email the forms over, and they can scan and email them back or just plop them in the mail.

I am willing to bet that 9 out of 10 will say to email it. Why? Because people today (especially boomers and seniors) realize how valuable their time left on this Earth is, and if there is some technology that can give them more time to do what they truly enjoy, then by gosh, they want to know more about it.

Now, don't misread all of this to think that relationships don't matter, because they do in most cases. The revolution I am referring to here is about altering the way you communicate, educate, and nurture new prospects.

For a small group of you, this will mean going completely digital, where you do all of your prospecting, marketing, and even selling over the phone and Internet from anywhere in the world.

However, for most of you, this book will teach you how to attract and nurture more new prospects than you ever imagined, all with the ultimate goal of getting them to see you face to face. The big difference is that I will be teaching you how to get prospects 100 percent sold on you before you even speak to them.

Even better is that you can be selling more than one person at the same time, 24 hours per day.

This revolution is about harnessing technology to alter your own personal lifestyle, giving you absolute control over your sales funnel, while at the same time enabling you to help more people, while making more money than you ever imagined possible.

You see, this revolution isn't just about your consumers and how they want to be educated and do business in today's world.

It is just as much about *you*, the entrepreneur. And I intend to show you in this book how you can become more of an authority and expert than you ever dreamed possible.

At the same time, I plan on showing you how to build a sales funnel that you not only control but also own. And this sales funnel is an asset that will serve you richly for years and be something you can sell down the road as well.

Before we get to the incredible story of financial advisor Steve Kennedy, let me tell you a brief story about myself.

Just four years ago, I was a complete digital dunce. I did not own a website, I didn't know what website hosting meant, I didn't know what a blog was or how it was created, and I had no idea what the term Search Engine Optimization (SEO) meant.

But I knew that I wanted to "go digital" when I saw how much momentum the Internet was building, not to mention that I had always been fascinated with online marketing and websites.

I began my digital marketing career buying my very first domain, www.AnnuityThinkTank.com. A couple of months and a couple thousand dollars later, my first site was live. And boy, was it horrible!

No lie, I actually started my site off with an all-black background, white font, and a bright pink logo (and bring pink accents). These were the three main colors of the site. And for those of you wondering why you never see websites with all-black backgrounds and white font, it is because it has probably caused more blindness than looking directly into the sun! It is simply brutal on the eyes.

This would just be the very first of my many website screw-ups over the next few years. My first 10 blogs had absolutely no tag words, there was no way for visitors to give me their information, I had a rotating banner that took up almost the entire home page (using hot pink as my primary color), pitiful headlines, and much, much more.

But what I wasn't afraid of doing was failing or testing things out. And over the course of the next two years, I spent well over $100,000 testing, rebuilding, hiring out SEO and web developer consultants, and building the brand and website, one painful day at a time.

And then, all of a sudden, it happened. The very first legitimate lead came in from my site. I can still recall the euphoria and excitement I had that day. You would have thought I won the lottery. From that day forward, I was hooked on Internet marketing.

Fast forward to today. I post content (blogs/video) and manage three different websites, I own over 650 domains, and my brother and I create anywhere from 300 leads (on slow months) to over 1,000 leads per month from our websites.

Needless to say, Internet marketing has changed my life. It has enabled me to make (and spend) a small fortune; it has given me the lifestyle to work from home and spend time with my growing family; it has enabled me to travel, live, and work anywhere that I want to be. Most importantly, it has enabled me to become a true entrepreneur that has complete control of my business, my leads, and my sales pipeline.

Now, some of you might be reading this and think that you could never do this. **Well, I am here to tell you that you can**. There was nothing special about me, except for the fact I had a burning desire to do smarter marketing, and I refused to give up.

In fact, that was the same trend that I now see with all of the financial advisors who have "gone digital" and have tremendous success. All of them failed at digital marketing on their first tries. One in particular (whom I am betting you have probably heard of) told me that he was within a week of giving up and going back to the traditional methods of marketing.

Still, you might be skeptical about digital marketing for some reason. So my aim in this book is to teach you how and why to do digital (aka Internet) marketing in your business.

Moreover, I want to show you exactly why the three points that I mentioned at the beginning of this chapter are so crucial to your growth, and even your existence, going forward.

And I plan on teaching you all of this in such a clear, rational, and implementable way that you take action and control of your own sales pipeline and make more money with a better lifestyle, all while helping more clients than you ever imagined possible.

Get ready for a huge transformation in your own business as you learn digital marketing from the captivating story of an entrepreneur who hits rock bottom before finally coming out of the abyss to accomplish things you won't believe.

Although the character Steve Kennedy in this story is fictional, I believe that you will find a bit of yourself in him throughout this adventure. Join him on his journey.

Welcome to the Digital Revolution facing all entrepreneurs and small business owners.

1

A DAY IN THE LIFE OF A FINANCIAL ADVISOR...

As I pulled out of my driveway at 6 o'clock in the morning, I could already feel myself getting anxious about the evening's event.

Although it would be a full 12 hours before I had to get in front of a group of boomers and seniors at my financial workshop seminar at Fleming's Prime Steakhouse near my office that night, I was already getting those nervous feelings in my stomach.

And it probably didn't help that the attendance was going to be worse than I had anticipated—especially after you consider that I had to mail an extra 1,250 mailers compared to last year just to keep the room at the ideal level of butts in the seats.

But the underlying problem was even bigger... I was losing my passion for doing these financial workshops. This was my eighth year in a row focused on seminar marketing, and I was quickly approaching burnout mode. To help with the issue, I made sure to always change up the entire seminar message every other year, and that did give me temporary relief each time.

Pulling into my office parking lot located in a nice area near downtown Winter Park, Florida, I noticed that Judy had already arrived. She was loading up her car with our projector and some of the boxes containing the handouts and client surveys. *What would I do without Judy?* I thought. Judy had been my loyal assistant for going on 14 years, and she really held this place together. In fact, she was the glue of the office more than I was most of the year.

"Good morning, Judy," I said as I hopped out of my 5-series silver BMW while grabbing my coffee mug and briefcase.

"Hey there, Steve. I know you hate getting bad news in the morning, but you have some fires to put out before your 9 a.m. appointment. Also, we had voicemails from two different couples who have canceled for tonight's workshop."

"Lovely," I exclaimed sarcastically. "Did they leave any reason why they can't make it, or was it the standard 'make sure to call our office at 10 p.m. when they knew they wouldn't have to speak to anyone's voicemail?"

"You guessed it," said Judy. "But the bigger issue is what I have sitting on your desk. Apparently, the Lyon family called up Jackson National and told the transfer team to permanently cancel the transfer paperwork on that $175,000 annuity, as they have changed their minds for some reason."

"You have to be kidding me. I spent hours meeting with the Lyons and even had their children on the phone, explaining exactly why this was a perfect fit with the rest of their retirement plan. I bet their skeptical daughter got to them. Did the Lyons even attempt to contact us about this, or did they go direct to the carrier and try to avoid talking to us about it?"

"They went direct to Jackson," said Judy.

"It's going to be one of those days, Judy. Since I can't call the Lyons to see if this deal is savable until later this morning, let me go through my emails, and then you and I can meet to go over the game plan for tonight's workshop."

I stomped into my office, wondering if it was possible to have a day start off any worse.

Seminar Pregame

"OK, so how many buying units do we have coming tonight, now that those two couples have backed out?" I asked Judy.

"Sixteen total buying units, which comes out to 29 total people coming. There were a handful of single seniors, and one of them is bringing his adult child to tag along. But I did look down the list to see our favorite plate-licking couple."

"Are you serious?" I interrupted. "The Harrisons are coming back for their third free meal! If they don't book an appointment this time, we are banning them from our workshops for life. I don't mind educating people, but this is ridiculous. Not to mention, I basically teach the same principles in every workshop, and they are just flat out taking advantage of the situation at this point."

"Agree completely. I will put a little pressure on them to make a decision either way," said Judy.

Scratching my head after doing some quick math, I asked, "So, Judy, this means that after you take out the Harrisons, we only have 15 total buying units for a seminar that is going to cost us $7,000 to put on.

"At some point in the very near future, these workshops are not going to make any financial sense. We keep having to send more and more mailers, the price of dinner gradually goes up, and it is a rare occasion when we can find a single couple that hasn't already been to at least one other dinner workshop like this in the past. I'm afraid that these financial workshops are just oversaturated down here in Florida."

"You could be right, Steve. But we always seem to get one or two new clients from each workshop, after it is all said and done. And since our average client is bringing assets of over $400,000 to us, they always seem to keep paying for themselves," said Judy.

"Yes, but after you factor in that I usually meet with the clients three times before they move any money over, and then it usually takes another 30 to 90 days to get all of their money transferred, and since I am now mostly fee-based, it takes me well over a year from the workshop to hit the break-even point... I just don't know how long I can keep doing this. There has to be a better way to market. Perhaps I can go back to our own direct mail postcards or use that other third-party group that mailed for us a few years ago."

"Steve, you do recall that we were getting less than a 0.5 percent response rate on those postcards before we finally threw in the towel?" Judy pointed out. "It would be like you getting back on the phone to cold call and getting hung up on by 99 out of 100 people you called. Talk about an archaic way to market!

"And don't forget why we canceled with that third-party mail house," she continued. "We had three times as many complaints from consumers, saying they felt like our message was misleading, than we did actual real responses." Let's fix our current marketing problems before we jump back into something we know wasn't working for us."

"Judy, sometimes I don't know what I would do without you," I said with a big smile.

"I know, Steve, I know."

But little did Judy know that I simply didn't enjoy doing seminars anymore. In fact, I hated them. When I first started out doing these financial workshops, I was alive with energy, and I really felt like I was giving some great value to everyone in the room.

But now, I felt like the entire thing was too staged. At times it even felt like I was a rancher, prodding cattle to come into my pen in hopes that I could find a couple of them prime and fat enough to "take to the market."

People today are much wiser about these workshops than they were just a few years ago. They know that they are going to be sold something, and they usually come in with their guard up and their salesman antennae at high mast. Not to mention all of the negative press in places like *AARP*, *Forbes*, and *The Wall Street Journal* about all of the reasons consumers should avoid financial workshops like the plague was putting a damper on these live events.

More importantly, I was losing faith in these workshops as I was having trouble believing they were truly the best way to get new clients, and not just because they were costing me more each year.

It had more to do with the fact that most of the baby boomers and retirees who came to these events didn't want to be sold this way. I sure knew I didn't want to be sold this way, either!

If I had a question or a problem that I needed solved, the first thing I did was start researching on the Internet. The last thing I did was wait by my mailbox hoping to get an invitation for a free dinner seminar that may or may not solve my problem.

I had faced the fact that there was a limited number of ideal prospects left here in Central Florida who wanted to meet a financial advisor this way, let alone wanted to get any kind of free education at a dinner event.

The problem was, I had no clue how else to effectively get new prospects. If someone could show me a better way, I would gladly forfeit late-night seminars in a heartbeat.

That reminded me, I needed to call my wife, Jen, before my day got crazy, as she was still asleep when I left the house. We had been fighting off and on for years about my late nights at work, and she hated these evening seminars more than anyone.

In fact, almost all of our fights over the past few years seemed to stem from me not being home at a decent hour. And there was a two-week period when I didn't make it home a single evening before 10 p.m. where I thought she was going to divorce me. Jen had grown up in a family where her father was home promptly at 5:15 p.m. for a sit-down dinner, and she expected the same of me. But unfortunately for her, I had a different job than her father, and I tried my best to constantly remind her that my hard work and long hours were what provided for our nice home and lifestyle.

My Other Love

"Hey, Jen, have the kids left for school yet?" I asked my wife. "I was hoping to tell them to have a great day."

"Steve, do you even remember what time their bus leaves?" she asked.

I could sense the hint of frustration and sarcasm in her voice. "Listen, Jen, I know you hate how many hours I have been working, but I am doing all of this for you and the kids. I promise that the long hours and late appointments and workshops will end soon. I just need a little more time to build up to where I need to be."

The line went silent on the other end as I waited for my wife to say something.

After a few awkward seconds, Jen, my wife of 17 years, slowly said something that I have never forgotten: "Steve, you tell the kids and me the same thing every year, but every year we feel like we see less of you. Good luck tonight. I hope all of this is worth missing your kids growing up." Then, she hung up the phone.

2

MEET FINANCIAL ADVISOR STEVE KENNEDY

I grew up in the Orlando, Florida area in a nice, middle-class family. My two brothers and I went to good public schools, had great friends and neighborhood kids our age, and always seemed to get the essential things we needed, like one big gift from Santa each year, clothes that didn't make us stand out as either too poor or too rich, and a family dinner each night where all five of us contributed to the conversation of what we did that day.

My father grew up in and around Central Florida and rarely left the state; he was quite the homebody who always claimed with his funny laugh, "The city might fall apart if I ever left town for very long."

He was a middle-management engineer for Disney in Orlando; he never got paid that well, but he was always home for dinner, he always had great stories to tell about the famous park, and we three boys all thought he could walk on water, since he could get us into Magic Kingdom or Epcot pretty much any time we wanted to go.

My dad was incredibly loyal. He worked at Disney his entire career, even though he only received two promotions throughout his 40 years with the company. However, looking back, I don't think my dad had the same kind of burning desire to do something big and make lots of money like I did. Being able to provide basic care for us, put a roof over our heads, pay the house off, make it home in time for dinner, and have a bit left over to save for retirement were his biggest priorities.

He did, however, have a Disney pension that kept a solid stream of money coming in long after his last day of work. In many cases, it made up for the promotions that he missed out on.

His lack of desire for nice things could have just been due to the fact that he was born in the early 1930s and watched his own parents struggle to get by and put food on the table sometimes. It seemed this so-called "Greatest Generation" really did know a thing or two about saving money and retiring with a lifetime income. Some days I wondered if I would have been better off just following his footsteps.

Regardless, his sense of peace and lack of anxiety about running out of money enabled me to know exactly what kind of retirement I wanted to build for my own baby boomer and senior clients today. In fact, I would tell the story of my dad who, out of his 40-year career, only broke the six-figure income mark for four years. Yet, he retired with no debt, a modest house that was paid for, updated cars, and a lifetime income from pension and Social Security that most Americans would be envious of today.

And the story had power, because most of the people that I spoke to and met with were making (or had made) well over single six-figures, so an ideal, worry-free retirement could be accomplished on smaller incomes. It just took persistent, consistent, and smart saving and investing.

If only I could find more prospects who had the same saving mentality as my father. Or perhaps, if I could only be a better marketer and find those ideal clients instead of having to always cut through so many countless bad leads to get one decent client those days. But that was an entirely different story.

When my father passed away in late 2012, it seemed as if the entire area of Orlando where we lived came to pay its respects. He was an honest man who had no enemies and always took an active role in church, Boy Scouts (he was a loyal Eagle Scout), the community, and his beloved Kiwanis club.

It was tough to say anything bad about my old pop, and we all missed him dearly.

My mother grew up in Virginia, where her father was stationed in the Navy. She started off teaching the second grade and then finally resigned to become a stay-at-home mom after giving birth to me, her first son, in October 1961. She was the most loving mother the three of us unruly boys could ask for. She knew exactly when we were up to no good and when to scold us, and she knew exactly when to love and encourage us.

Mom was really the soul of the household, both in her strong spiritual beliefs and influence and in her never-ending energy. She was active in our local church, her garden club where she chatted and hung out with the other local stay at home mothers, and any other club or philanthropic group that was helping out the local community in and around Orlando.

After Dad's death, she ended up selling the home that we grew up in and downgrading into a large one-bedroom condo that was just a block away from my youngest brother and his wife, who both lived in Orlando. My brother was an executive with the Golf Channel, and his wife stayed at home with their two kids. She was a huge help to my mother whenever she needed any assistance.

My middle brother was kind of the wild child of the group. He had yet to marry and had no kids that we knew of. He had a handsome paycheck coming in every month from his employer, Patagonia, out in Ventura, California, which enabled him to take nonstop personal "bucket-list" trips abroad and make us all a bit envious.

When he did find the time to make it home for the holidays, his stories of running with bulls, skydiving in Peru, scuba diving in the Amazon river, and bungee jumping off of anything that seemed like a challenge did keep the family entertained for hours.

As for me, I was always a decent student my entire life, but most of my time, energy, and passion were spent on a field. Throughout elementary and high school, I was one heck of a baseball player, and like most teenage boys who were all-stars in their own city but had no idea how competitive it was in the real world, I had big dreams to make it to the major leagues one day.

Sadly (or really fortunately, in hindsight), I suffered two broken fingers on my throwing hand my senior year while colliding with the catcher on a wild play at home plate (where I ended up being safe), and my chances of going pro went out the window.

But in reality, it was a blessing in disguise, as I had no idea what I wanted to do with my life. In fact, I hadn't even applied to any colleges; I was just making assumptions that I would get some kind of full or partial baseball scholarship to a small school where I could work my way up into the majors.

So, after getting harassed by both of my parents to apply to basically every college in Florida, I was finally accepted (at the last minute before graduating high school) into a local Orlando school that had recently changed its name to University of Central Florida (UCF).

At UCF, I majored in business management and basically went through the motions my first year. I mostly recall learning about beer, girls, and how to manage my life and budget without help from my parents, even though they were incredibly close by and I frequently went home for a warm meal on Sundays.

But after an elective in finance that I wasn't even that excited about taking, I came alive at school for the first time that I could recall. I loved finance and economics, so much so that I decided to get a second major in finance. Investing and learning how and why the economy acted and reacted at any given point in time always fascinated me. So after just a couple of finance classes, I knew for the first time in my adult life what industry I wanted to be in.

After graduating somewhere in the middle of my class at UCF, I ended up taking a job at Bankers Life and Casualty, where they groomed and educated me on how to become an insurance salesman.

The first year was full of training, harassing friends and family to buy any kind of insurance from me, countless hours of cold calling (this was before the do-not-call rules came into play, so I could just go down the phone book, which I am embarrassed to say that I did on occasion), and even some door-to-door knocking.

It was a tough start, but I still cherish those days, as they taught me not only how to cut my teeth as a salesman, but, just as importantly, how not to ever sell again once I built some real momentum.

After eight solid years at Bankers as an insurance specialist, I realized that my personality and my personal goals were pushing me to do something bigger and better—not to mention the fact that I really wasn't cut out to be a corporate guy who drank the Banker's Kool-Aid, and I simply couldn't do another one of those rah-rah conferences where the executives did nothing but brag about themselves and what the company was doing, adding little value to us as producers. So I resigned on good terms and went out to start my own company, which I called Kennedy Insurance Services, LLC.

My Family

After meeting my wife through a mutual friend shortly after I started at Bankers, we knew almost right away that we were going to get married.

Jennifer (Jen) brought much-needed stability and structure into my life, similar to my mother back when I was under her roof. She, too, was a teacher at a local elementary school in the Orlando area, but we both knew that she would most likely leave her teaching job and raise our children when that time came.

Just a few short years after marriage, we introduced our beautiful daughter Ashley Kennedy to the world. For me, having a young daughter was like falling in love all over again, and it was shortly after her birth that I had this burning desire to provide much better for my growing family.

And because Bankers was taking more than half my commissions, regardless of how much time, energy, or money I personally put in to generate the new client, I realized that I was never going to get rich or have any control if I was under their umbrella. So, off I went on the never-ending journey of an independent financial professional.

Two and a half years after Ashley's birth, my wife and I were grateful to bring Stephen Kennedy Jr. into the world. Not only did he give my wife one of the most uncomfortable pregnancies I have ever heard of, he also decided to come out quite early, which caused my wife and me to spend about 20 days in the hospital before we finally came home with little Steve. Needless to say, my wife ordered me to "man surgery" to make sure we never had to go through a pregnancy like that again.

The Evolution of My Practice as an Independent Producer

As I mentioned, my very first company that I registered in the state of Florida was named Kennedy Insurance Services, LLC. I was young, clueless on how to set up anything or name anything correctly, and had no idea what I was getting myself into.

After saying goodbye to my job at Bankers, I quickly realized that I also said goodbye to many positive things, such as my insurance renewals (for some reason my thinking was that I was still entitled to my renewals), paying for my CE (Continuing Education) credits and annual license fees, and even paying for my E&O (Errors & Omission) insurance. Turns out Bankers did provide some nice perks I took for granted.

With all of these upfront costs, including the filing of the LLC and getting my company licensed with the state as well, I was going backward quickly, with absolutely no income coming in at all. This kind of pressure, combined with the frequent reminders from a wife at home trying to buy our groceries, diapers, and clothes for the kids that we didn't have enough money, was enough to get me moving fast.

I quickly went out and visited some of my old clients; I joined the local chamber of commerce to do some networking; and I got back on the phone and started dialing for dollars.

After finally building some momentum and closing some cases, I realized that I needed to seriously work on a real marketing plan. Relying on the phone was not only risky, it also wasn't enjoyable to wedge and force my way into getting an appointment with someone who clearly couldn't wait to hang up on me.

In fact, I would say that at least 4 out of 10 people I spoke to hung up on me, three more quickly said they weren't interested and to never call back, and the other three listened to my pitch (probably to give them time to think of a good excuse to refuse) and then politely told me, "No, thanks." I could only book an appointment one time for every 50 calls. This was no way to run a business.

In my quest to find a good marketing system, I met another insurance agent at a chamber of commerce networking event who really "sold" me on annuities for the first time. Of course, I knew about annuities, since we had them at Bankers, and they were something we had to know to pass the insurance exam, but I had never thought about selling them before.

But this local agent encouraged me to go to a free annuity event in Orlando that was being hosted by Allianz Life. And when I heard that they gave out three free CE credits just for attending, I was all-in.

I still recall going home from the Allianz event with so much excitement that I could hardly contain myself. Not only did they have some of the best-selling fixed and equity-indexed annuities in the country, they also had annuities with 10 percent bonuses to the client up front.

I couldn't wait to get on the phone again to tell people about this exciting news. I couldn't imagine anyone telling me "no" if I could give them a 10 percent up-front bonus. However, I realized quickly that I should probably learn a bit more about how the rest of the annuity worked before I started selling them.

Upon appointing with (otherwise known as signing up to be able to sell a certain insurance carrier's products) Allianz Life and a handful of other carriers, I immediately received a phone call from a company called Asset Marketing, out of California, which was going to educate me and help me sell these equity-indexed annuities.

After a few phone calls with one of their internal wholesalers, I was ready to try out my luck with some phone prospects. Needless to say, with all of the excitement of the new product with the tantalizing bonus, I completely forgot about my quest to find a solid marketing method. I mean, who needs marketing when you had a bonus to sell?

Little did I know how wrong I was.

Not to bore you with all of the fine details, but I did end up becoming a pretty darn good annuity salesman. In my first year, I added an extra $1.1 million of total fixed indexed annuity sales on top of my average year of life insurance cases (keep in mind that this was back when equity-indexed annuities were paying a 13 percent commission).

After a few years of getting the annuity pitch down well, I was on my way to breaking through the $5-million-in-one-year mark, and I seemed to rarely even talk about life insurance any more.

This also enabled me to finally hire my first full-time assistant, an incredibly reliable and hardworking middle-aged widow named Judy. She started working part-time with me a couple of years earlier whenever I needed help with a workshop or direct mail blast (where I would actually send all mail from my office to save money by cutting out the mail house).

And when the financial collapse of 2008–2009 hit, my little practice really took off. As more and more people wanted nothing to do with the market and knew they needed protection and lifetime income, I was the guy in town who had a really good story.

Not to mention, my entire slogan revolved around the statement, "Not a single one of my clients lost a penny in the financial collapse because of any product they bought from me. Could your Edward Jones or Morgan Stanley advisor say the same thing?" I would ask this of all of my prospects.

But even though I was making more money than I ever had at any point in my life, I was still running around like a chicken with its head cut off. My business was still running me, and I had no control of my sales pipeline, as all of my leads were produced by third-party platforms, including my seminar presentation that I was essentially "renting" from an insurance marketing company known as an FMO. Moreover, I did a pitiful job of doing what I originally intended from a financial perspective, which was to create my own personal annuity with residual commission income from my sales.

Finally, after the 05-50 scare back in 2005, when FINRA (Financial Industry Regulatory Authority) issued a notice to all broker dealers mandating that they declare these equity-indexed annuities that I was selling as securities, I saw what I considered the inevitable writing on the wall: These now-called "fixed-indexed annuities" would be under attack to become securities until Wall Street eventually got its way. And when the 151A notice came out in the last few weeks of December 2010, I vowed the following things as my 2011 New Year's resolutions:

- I would study and get my series 65 license before the last day of March 2011.
- I would start doing assets under management (AUM), along with annuities and life insurance to start building up a residual income.
- I would finally stop relying on and chasing around third-party marketing companies and build a marketing system where I actually had some control over my own most crucial piece of business: my sales and lead pipeline.

Wildly enough, I was able to achieve 2 out of my 3 New Year's resolutions by June of 2012.

I passed my series 65 less than 60 days after the New Year. I joined a great registered investment advisor (RIA) that not only approved all of my outside business activities, like fixed indexed annuities and indexed universal life, but also let me get full payouts on anything outside of AUM.

I changed my company name from Kennedy Insurance to Kennedy Financial Services, started filing as an S Corporation, and had big dreams for my new, improved small firm going forward.

And on the AUM side, I started capturing more, if not all, of my clients' assets. I was still able to use annuities and life insurance where needed, and I was finally on my way to creating a residual income stream as I quickly captured almost $7 million into AUM just by going back to my old clients.

Overall, I was feeling great about my business and was very optimistic that this could be the breakout year that I had been working so hard to build up to.

Of course, the one goal of the three I was still unable to fulfill was the marketing side of things.

However, I had a seminar mailer from my FMO that was pulling some incredible responses from consumers in my area and was able to fill up seminar rooms to standing room only (as Central Florida was loaded with older boomers and retirees who would come to these dinner events at the drop of a hat), I had a 30-minute radio show each Saturday morning on a great AM radio station in Orlando, and I could really see this practice taking off and enabling me to finally gain control of my business and spend more time with my family.

Little did I know that this marketing plan, or actually the lack of a real plan, would be my Achilles' heel for years to come.

3

LIFE AT HOME

It was already 9:30 by the time the last couple left that night's seminar. After breaking everything down, packing up, squaring away loose ends with the restaurant, and a 15-minute drive home, I figured I wouldn't get to see my two kids at all, who usually went to bed around 10 o'clock.

As my mind wandered to my last conversation with my irritated wife, who ended up hanging up on me, I realized someone was calling my name.

"Steve. Steve, snap out of it," said Judy. "The last couple just left, so let's clean this place up and hit the road."

Quickly coming back to reality, I said, "Well, that went better than I thought it would. Looks like six of the couples booked appointments."

"Yep," said Judy. "We know that 1 out of 6 will cancel or no-show, and half will just not be an ideal fit for us or perhaps just won't have any money and will be looking for some kind of miracle worker, so that leaves us with two or three potential new clients."

As I listened to Judy break down the numbers, I started to think about how sad it was that all of the time and money to put on a workshop came down to this. That after spending a few thousand dollars for printing, another $2,000 for food and to rent out almost the entire Fleming's Steakhouse (all well in advance of me ever recouping a single dollar), I was left here with two or three potential new prospects.

And the really sad part was how I was actually convincing myself that it wasn't so bad. I felt like I did back in college when I would overdrink and have the worst hangover of my life every Sunday, but by Tuesday I would convince myself that it wasn't so bad after all. And then by the following Friday, I would be back on a two-day bender with my fraternity brothers to do the entire cycle over again.

How was it that some financial advisors had figured out how to grow large practices without having to do these dreaded workshops their entire careers? How was it that some financial advisors were able to control their entire sales processes and funnels and didn't have to rely on third-party vendors like I did? I was even hearing about these "digital financial advisors" who were working from home with little to no overhead and still bringing in more business than I was.

I would give anything to be able to work from home, even just a couple of days a week. It would finally give me time to enjoy my children, and it certainly would take some pressure off of the tense relationship with my wife.

Deep down, I loved my family more than anything else in the world. But each year our expenses at home continued to climb because we upgraded houses, we upgraded cars, our daughter's clothes and miscellaneous expenses to "fit in" were out of control, and our son had taken up one of the most expensive sports known to man... golf.

Each passing year, I vowed to make more money with less busy work so that I could spend more time involved in building a strong relationship with my family.

But just the opposite seemed to happen. I kept finding myself in a vicious circle of putting out fires to save clients and having to spend more money for marketing and advertising to get in front of prospects, all while watching my time away from home get worse, not better.

Well, at least it was Thursday, and although I would be home shortly to find my entire family asleep, that weekend should end up being a great one to make up with Jen.

I had already promised her that there would be no working this weekend, and we even had a date night planned the following evening, when the kids would stay with Jen's mom, who lived nearby. And quite frankly, we both needed some time alone, as we hadn't gone on a real date night in well over a year.

4

RADIO ~~WAVES~~ TYPHOON

Judy and I kicked off that beautiful Friday morning by reviewing all of the couples that had booked appointments with us the night before. We had a ritual to personally call all of them the following day to thank them for attending and remind them about their upcoming appointment, what to expect, what to bring, and to see if they had any questions or concerns in particular that I could answer before we met.

Although it always ended up eating up most of my day after an event, prospects regularly told us how nice it was to feel like we cared about them with the next-day phone call.

After speaking to all of the couples but one, I was ready to call it a day and head home a bit early to surprise Jen and the kids. And then Judy came in and hit me with it.

"You won't believe this!" she said. "I just received a call from the radio station, and they are not only selling the station to some huge international media group, but they are also going to almost triple the cost of our airtime. Apparently the new owners feel that there are already too many financial shows on during the weekend, so they are going to see who really wants it and who doesn't. We have until Monday to decide."

"Can they do this legally?" I asked.

"Yes, I asked the same thing, and apparently the fine print that we signed says that if there is ever a complete sell or takeover of the station, the new group has full rights to change any and all contracts. They told me that, otherwise, no group would ever buy them if they were legally stuck in all of the old contracts."

I could begin to feel some sweat beads at the top of my head as my anger started to boil out of control. I had regularly paid this radio station just under $2,000 per week for my one-hour radio show (and my "complimentary" 30-second advertisements that were run throughout the week) for over two years. I paid them well over $200,000, and now they were kicking me to the curb as if I was some kind of bum.

Not to mention, my radio show was responsible for approximately 50 percent of my overall business and branding. *What am I going to do?* I thought.

"Judy, please get me Drew Connor's direct number at the station. I am not giving up without a fight," I said.

Drew Connor was the vice president of media sales for the radio company that I paid a king's ransom in media buys to over the last couple of years. He was also the one who came to my office in Orlando, looked me in the eye, and said they would never jack up the prices like this.

And although I fully realized that this price hijacking was occurring due to a takeover, it still didn't make it right in my eyes.

After Judy brought me the number, I dialed it as quickly as I could, still wondering how I was going to keep my cool in this phone call. I had learned the hard way that it never pays to lose your temper in situations like this, but my emotions were so frayed that it was going to be tough to resist telling Drew and his good-for-nothing company off.

"I need to speak to Drew, please," I said sternly after his assistant picked up the call.

"I'm sorry, but Drew is in a meeting right now. Can I have him return your call when he gets out?"

"This is an emergency. Is there any way that you can interrupt his meeting and tell him that Steve Kennedy really needs to speak to him?" I asked.

"Sorry, Steve, but Drew has asked us not to disturb him in this meeting. If you can give me your phone number, I will make sure Drew calls you today."

As I hung up the phone, all I could do was wonder how in the world I would make up the lead volume that the radio show produced for me. Not only that, it gave me some huge credibility as "that retirement guy on the radio," a nickname I had been called by a few referrals and clients in the past.

But what was really hitting me hard was the realization that I had little control of my most important asset in my company: my lead-prospecting funnel.

It was one thing to pay a third party for solid leads, but I never realized how vulnerable and out of control I was until I got the rug pulled out from under me. Suddenly, I started thinking about the future of the marketing company whose seminar system I had used exclusively for the past year. What if that company was sold or decided to take away the system for some reason?

At this moment, sweating and angry at my desk on a late Friday afternoon, I came to the realization that I had no control at all of my business. In fact, I had somehow let my business run me, and it took this radio typhoon ruining my day for me to realize this tough fact.

I had to make some changes, but first I really needed to speak to Drew to find out if there was any way to salvage things. After waiting another 30 minutes and trying to keep my mind off of the bad news (with no luck), I decided to send him an email, demanding he call me as soon as possible.

I looked down at my watch and realized it was already 3:45 in the afternoon. I promised my wife that I would be home early to relax and spend time with the kids before our big date night. She was going to kill me if I didn't show up at the house soon.

I decided to make another call to Drew, as I just couldn't get my mind off of the radio news that had altered my business future in the last few hours.

"Hey, this is Steve Kennedy again. I am really sorry to bother you again, but is Drew out of the meeting? I really need to talk with him before I leave today, and I am over here on the East Coast a few hours ahead of you," I said, attempting to give any excuse possible to get him on the phone.

"Mr. Kennedy," his assistant said, "he is coming out of the meeting now, and he promises to call you in five minutes."

Promises? I thought. *I also remember him promising never to leave me high and dry in our contract. Let's hope he actually calls in five minutes, or I might as well spend the rest of the afternoon meeting with a divorce lawyer, since my wife is going to be livid.*

After what felt like an hour, but was really only seven minutes, Judy was buzzing my line to let me know that she was sending Drew through.

I started talking immediately before he could get a word in. "Drew, what the heck is going on, man! You guys decide to sell the company without mentioning a word to your loyal clients like me. Then, you don't even have the balls to call me directly, instead choosing to relay the message that a new group is going to triple our costs for the exact same radio time to my assistant? What kind of businessman are you?"

There was a slight hesitation on the line, and then Drew softly spoke. "Steve, I am not happy about these changes, either. I knew that the current owners of the station were not 100 percent happy, but I really did not have any idea that this deal was going down until this week. If it makes you feel any better, I just found out an hour ago that I no longer have a job once this deal is complete in a couple of weeks," he said.

My anger suddenly subsided, and I truly felt bad for what I said. I hated to see any family man lose his job, and it made it worse that I had just questioned his business ethics. "Man, I am really sorry Drew. I was so caught up thinking that this was some big conspiracy against us small guys that I never even considered that you and your staff might be impacted as well. But, can you tell me if there is any way to save my spot at the current price? Is there anyone else there I can speak to about an exception? This decision can really make or break my practice."

"I'm sorry, Steve, this is out of my control. Trust me, if I had any leverage at all, I would try to save my job and the radio spots of great customers like you. But this is a done deal, and the new owners couldn't care less about me, or a majority of the small to midsized accounts like you.

"They purchased our station for the big corporate accounts who spend upward of $100,000 per month, and they are going to just squeeze the small guys by overcharging you in order to free up more ideal airtime to sell to the corporate accounts where most of the big money is. I am really sorry that it all went down this way, Steve. I wish you the best of luck."

"Ditto, Drew. Let me know if I can help out in any way in terms of recommendations for your new job."

"Thank you," Drew said. We both hung up, realizing that neither of us really had much control in this situation.

And although I wasn't losing my job like Drew, I could find myself in some hot water if I didn't find a solution for more leads to replace my radio show lead flow quickly. But none of it was going to matter if I didn't get home for my long-overdue date night with Jen.

I picked up my briefcase and shuffled past Judy, wishing her a great weekend and reassuring her that we would find a solution to this mess next week. I hopped in my BMW and floored it to get home before all of the bad Friday rush hour traffic.

5

DATE NIGHT

When I walked inside our house at 4:45, I could already smell my wife's perfume in the air. It was one of those scents that instantly took my mind back to our early days of marriage when we had date nights. It was the same perfume that Jen always sprayed on her wrist and into her hair before any big date night. Sadly, she still had the same bottle after all of these years, as we were rarely able to do date nights anymore due to my busy schedule and the kids' activity-filled weekends.

Although this sweet smell reminded me of some great times, it also reminded me that she was showered, dressed, ready to go, and most likely fuming about why I was late to arrive home after a promised early arrival.

I slowly peeked into our bedroom and wondered if I was going to see a hairbrush flying at my face or just hear verbal abuse. Then, my jaw dropped.

Sitting on our bed with a glass of red wine was the most elegant, beautiful woman I had ever laid eyes on. It was as if Jen looked 10 years younger than when I last saw her, just 24 hours before. She was glowing in a tight-fitting black dress that cut off just enough below her shoulders to show off a little cleavage, four-inch black heels, and her hair styled just like she used to have it back when we met.

"Wow," was all I could muster, as I looked my beautiful wife up and down. "You look amazing, babe. I am so sorry about being late. You have no idea what kind of day I had at the office."

"Steve, let's just enjoy the evening. And promise me that we won't have to talk about your work tonight, and the lateness will all be forgotten. I really just want to have an uninterrupted date night with the man I fell in love with years ago," Jen said with a cute look.

I went in to give her a kiss on the cheek (I knew better than to ruin a woman's lipstick before making it out of the house) and told her that I needed 15 minutes to shower and get ready, and then I would join her downstairs for a glass of wine before we headed off to dinner.

La Luce

As the valet opened the door for my wife, I could see all of his other college-aged buddies looking over to admire my incredible-looking wife. I truly was a lucky man, and although the radio catastrophe was still heavy on my mind, I couldn't help but be thankful for marrying such a beautiful, caring wife.

This evening was special, not just because it was a much-needed night alone but because it was also the same restaurant where we celebrated our engagement over 20 years earlier. The restaurant we were at for probably the fourth time in 20 years was called La Luce, and it had the best Italian food in all of Central Florida, in my humble opinion.

I called in to book the reservation a couple of weeks earlier when we both decided we desperately needed a date night, and being the salesman that I was, I convinced them to give us the VIP booth in the back with all of the privacy.

And even though my day began as one of the worst of the year, I had a good feeling it was going to end well with our date.

As we were ushered back to our private table by the maître d', I heard a male voice calling out my name.

"Hey, Steve. Looking good, man."

As I looked over to see who was yelling my name loud enough for everyone in the area to turn their heads, I saw one of my long-time clients whom I really enjoyed working with, Paul Heller. He had his wife with him, whom I had only met a couple of times, and the two of them, both in their mid-60s, seemed to be having a good time; I noticed that they just had another bottle of wine brought to their table.

"Great to see you, Paul; great to see you, Debbie. Do you both remember my wife, Jen?"

"Of course," said Paul without hesitation. "How could we forget a purty thing like your wife? Why do you think we invested our money with you?"

There was laughter from all four of us, but the loudest chuckle certainly came from Paul.

We made some small talk for a bit, and then Paul hit me with an innocent question, reminding me of what I was trying so hard to forget about tonight on my date.

"Hey, Steve. How is that radio show of yours going? I always love to refer my golf buddies over to you, telling them to listen to my main man on the biggest AM station in Orlando," said Paul.

Without thinking, I quickly said, "It's going great."

After my reply, I became quiet, and my hungry and somewhat impatient wife finally excused us, and we told the Hellers how great it was to see them.

I spent the next 10 minutes trying to justify in my mind why I lied to a client about my radio show. I felt bad about not telling him the truth, and now I couldn't get the thought of the radio contract out of my head.

In fact, I avoided telling anyone, as the only person in my circle who knew was Judy. Perhaps I thought that the longer I didn't tell anyone, the better the chance that the radio station's purchase would fall apart.

For many reasons, I just didn't want to admit that this was happening to my business. It was actually embarrassing how flawed my small business was to rely on a source that I had absolutely no control of for 50 percent of my entire sales pipeline.

Even though I was conversing with my wife, she could tell that something was distracting me, that I wasn't 100 percent into our conversation.

And then, all of a sudden, Jen said to me, "Let's hear it. What is eating away at your brain? I have known you for too long to know when something is weighing on your mind. Let's just get it out on the table so we can enjoy the rest of the evening."

Wondering if I should even open this can of worms on our long-awaited date night or just wait till we got home, my mind got the best of me, and I finally blurted out with no filter whatsoever, "My radio show has come to an end, the bastards sold the company, and I will be losing about half of my new prospects each month going forward."

I looked at Jen and could tell she didn't grasp the enormity of what I was saying. This was most likely because we rarely talked about my business, my marketing, or how I got new prospects.

At the end of the day, all she cared about was that we could pay our mortgage, she could spend whatever she needed to on groceries, go on her semiannual shopping spree at the outlet malls, and we take our annual week trip to Destin, Florida. As long as there was money in the bank, she frankly never asked anything about my job.

Perhaps this was just another reason we needed to talk more. The more I thought about it, the issue was that we rarely talked at all anymore. The conversations we had were usually about the kids and why I was hardly ever home to do things with her and our children.

While she continued to stare at me, not knowing exactly what to say, I blurted out, "This is a very big deal, Jen. This could drastically change how much I make, how much you get to spend, and it could affect our already embarrassing retirement savings."

"Can't you just do some other marketing to replace the radio? Wasn't that eating up a bunch of your marketing budget anyway?" asked Jen.

Well, at least she listened to me in the past about something—I was shocked she remembered the conversation we had a year earlier about my radio costs.

"Unfortunately, it isn't that easy. And if it were, every one of my competitors would be doing that kind of marketing as well. Either way, I am really sorry to drop all of this on you during our date night. I just found out about it today, and that was the reason I was late coming home. I had to speak to the vice president of the station to see if this was all true. Turns out, he is getting laid off because of this deal as well. The whole thing really stinks," I said.

Jen was looking at me a little more seriously now, and she said, "Steve, does this mean that you are going to be around me and the kids even less and that you are going to be even more stressed out when you are home? If so, I don't know how much longer I can take this. I mean, this is getting ridiculous... we married each other so that we could build a family, come even closer together as a couple, and see each other more than we did living apart. Yet, the only time we spend together seems to be mending our relationship on the weekends. And that is on a good weekend."

I sat there with a gut-wrenching feeling in my stomach, and I didn't know if I was going to tear up or puke, because she was hitting me right between the eyes; and I knew deep down that everything she said was true.

"Steve, I love you. I really do. The kids love you and look up to you. You have provided for us for so many years, and we can't tell you how thankful we are for that. But every year around Christmas, you tell us that the next year is going to be different. That you are going to have your best year ever and that you will be able to spend more time with us. Yet, every year that never happens. You continue to grow your business, which is great, but you don't have anything or any time left for us, and we simply don't believe you anymore when you say things are changing for the better."

Jen continued, "I want to believe you, I really do. And I really didn't have any intention on spilling all of this out on you tonight. I was hoping that tonight could be kind of a rebirth for our marriage, and that we could start doing date nights like this more often. But as soon as I could tell that all you could think about was work tonight, I had to say something.

"The kids and I agree that we would rather have a smaller house, downgrade our nice cars, and spend less just to have you around more. It isn't all about the money, Steve. And no radio show should ever be so important that you would neglect your wife on a date night that we needed for our marriage more than anything. This work obsession has to change. Or at least find a way to get it on autopilot, like you've always talked about doing."

It's a good thing that we have the private booth, I thought. Here we were, two grown adults, both crying and not enjoying any of the nice bottle of wine we ordered.

We finished the dinner with some small talk about what the kids were up to in school, and then we grabbed the check and called it an early night. The ride home was one of the most silent rides that I had ever taken, as we both reflected on the conversation that just happened at dinner.

As for me, it was time for change, and perhaps this radio show catastrophe was really a blessing in disguise. But either way, I was going to make my business work, get more control of my sales funnel, and spend a whole heck of a lot more time with my wife and kids. I couldn't afford to lose my wife and kids; no amount of leads or success could replace them for me.

6

THE WHALE

The rest of my weekend actually turned out great. Jen's sharp remarks hit their target, and I spent so much time loving and really getting to know my kids that they probably wondered what happened to their old dad.

My wife and I laid out some family ground rules, including one stating that we would have a mandatory date night once per month; and now that the radio show was ending my weekend work, I had no excuse not to be at every one of the kids' sporting events on the weekends.

And as crazy as it sounds, I was actually quite happy with the family ground rules, because I clearly needed a blueprint and some rules in place to keep me as active as I needed to be with my family. Sometimes work, money, and my competitive nature could blind me to just how many hours I worked and how much control my job had on me.

I finally set my mind on gaining back control of my job, family time, and happiness. The big question that I still needed to answer was how to incorporate marketing and a system for my business that could help me run more on autopilot.

Basically, I needed to be less involved in everything and find a way to get some processes in place so I could focus on my passions and what I was good at.

Monday Back at the Office

Despite not knowing exactly what I was going to do with my marketing, and despite the fact that I was going to have to officially cancel my radio contract that day, I came into the office the following Monday with some newfound energy.

I walked in with a big smile on my face and said to Judy, "Well, today we begin again. Get me the form that I need to sign to cancel the radio show, and let's cut ties and say goodbye to radio in this office."

"Already on your desk, Steve. I knew that there was no way that you were ever going to pay that outrageous amount to be on air. You might not be afraid to spend money on marketing, but I have known you long enough to know that you won't flush it down the toilet," said Judy.

We both laughed. Judy knew me all too well.

Back at my desk, I started to review my calendar, hoping to find some time to do some Internet searches for new marketing platforms for financial advisors like me. I noticed that one of the couples from Thursday's seminar was already on the books for this morning. "Excellent," I said to myself.

When they booked that quickly, it was usually a strong sign that they had a problem or financial pain that they were dealing with. What I found was that my seminar attendees who booked appointments the quickest either had no money and were hoping that I was the "Money Messiah" who could create a miracle with the lack of money they saved for retirement, or they were quite wealthy and didn't hesitate to make moves. *Let's hope for the latter.*

The great news was that I had about an hour and a half before my first appointment with this new couple. Time to surf the web in search of my radio prospecting replacement.

My first search yielded a bunch of cookie-cutter website marketing platforms with drip emails that I didn't exactly believe in. I was smart enough to know that my clients and ideal prospects were on the Internet, but I was also smart enough not to bet the farm on finding new prospects online. It just seemed like there were too many scammers pitching everything from SEO, to Internet leads, to email marketing that just didn't seem proven to me.

If it were as easy to generate great prospects online as some of these "Internet gurus" claimed, then why wasn't every financial advisor doing it?

My next search on helping financial professionals with marketing yielded a bunch of different FMO offers. I saw great success with my FMO's seminar presentation and platform, so I wasn't completely ready to jump ship.

For the next search, I looked for direct mail experts, as I had seen some pretty good success with direct mail in the past. Unfortunately, all of the legitimate-looking direct mail houses that specialized in helping financial advisors only offered seminar mailers, and I already had a great seminar mailer.

What I needed was a good direct mail piece that got baby boomers' attention and had them raise their hands to speak to me without having to go to an actual seminar. But the more I searched for this kind of direct mail piece, the more I realized that it was like finding water in a desert… it just didn't exist without the postcard being completely misleading or some bait-and-switch tactic. And I was not about to stoop to that.

All of a sudden, I looked at my computer screen's clock and realized it was just four minutes until this new couple arrived. I thought, *Wow, time really flies when you are searching for something specific on the web!*

I pulled out the client feedback form they filled out on Thursday, and it didn't really tell me that much. They answered the questions but were very ambiguous. I was already starting to wonder if this couple was going to be another one of those seminar prospects pleading with me to pull magical retirement money out of my hat.

My office intercom buzzed as Judy gave the heads-up that the couple was pulling up in the parking lot. And although I usually didn't ask this question, as there were typically clients or prospects in the office, I asked Judy, "What kind of car are they driving?"

"One of those Buick SUVs. I think it is called the Encore," Judy replied.

"Probably not the rich clients I was hoping for," I said under my breath.

But at least they didn't get dropped off in a taxi like that one nightmare couple that came in hoping for Miracle Steve to wave his retirement wand. They showed up with a statement showing all of their retirement assets at $11,000, and they were hoping to retire and receive at least $1,200 per month for the rest of their lives. By the way, they were both 64 years old.

Judy softly knocked on my closed office door and led the Smiths in. They were dressed like conservative Floridian seniors on their way to an all-you-can-eat buffet, and they appeared to be close to 70.

I reached out and politely shook hands with both Mr. and Mrs. Smith, introduced myself while making sure to flash my signature smile, and then asked them to be seated and make themselves at home.

I started the conversation off very low key to get to know them, to see if we were a fit together, and to fish for any problems or pain that I could uncover.

"Thanks again for coming in for a consultation. I hope you received some value from the seminar last Thursday?"

"Yes, we did," said Larry Smith. "In fact, we have been to at least six other dinner events like this with other financial professionals, and you are the first one who impressed us so much that we booked an appointment. Your explanation on estate taxes and estate loopholes was the main reason that we wanted to come in right away. No financial advisor has ever told us about that. Even the ones that we paid in the past."

My initial reaction of thinking this couple might be just an average prospect immediately changed. I had yet to meet someone whose main objective was to save as much money as possible on estate taxes who didn't have a large estate.

That was the entire reason I always spent 15 minutes going over the most powerful estate-planning loopholes and potholes in my presentation... to get the attention of any wealthy people in the room.

I went into my proven opening sentence:

"Thanks, I am really glad to hear that you received some great information from my presentation. And I really want to thank you for coming in today to see if there is anything that I can help you with. I don't really know if I am the advisor who can solve all of your problems, and I certainly don't know if I am the best choice for you as a financial planner. But the only way that we can both find out if I can be of some help is for me to ask you a few questions. Do you mind if I ask a few questions about you guys first?"

"Of course. That would be great, Steve," replied Larry confidently.

I asked the couple some easy questions about how they met, where they grew up, what they did for a living, and a few nonfinancial inquiries to get them talking. I found that most people never bought a financial plan or financial product without getting comfortable and building a relationship first.

And the few times I skipped this relationship-building step, I either never converted the prospect to a client, or it took me much longer because I had to reel them back in, compared to me just taking the time to do it correctly on the front end.

It turned out that the Smiths both grew up in Southern California, started dating their junior year of high school, and ended up splitting ways when Debbie got accepted to school at UNC-Chapel Hill, while Larry stayed in state and attended University of Southern California.

The two stayed in touch and remained friends over the next four years, and after graduation, they both found themselves working in Florida.

Larry was in Lakeland, Florida working for a somewhat new company at the time called Publix Supermarkets, where he was hired on as a warehouse and shipping consultant.

Debbie was fortunate to grab an engineering job at the large Florida utility company called Florida Power and Light, based out of South Florida.

After a few meetings on weekends, the two started dating again. Before they knew it, they were both asking their companies to be relocated to Central Florida, where the two would attempt to meet in the middle.

Shortly after, they decided to get married and start a family in a city called Kissimmee, just outside of Orlando.

When Larry began telling me the story of how he eventually left Publix to start his own logistics company to focus on shipping and distribution for retailers and grocers, I could already tell that this couple was not the typical couple that came into my office.

Although he hadn't revealed their financial issues or how much money they had saved up, I had an intuition that it was a nice sum. I guess what they say is correct about never judging a couple's bank account by the vehicle they pull up in.

Larry finished up the story by revealing that he sold his company a few years earlier for a little over $12 million and that he and Debbie fired their Merrill Lynch broker years earlier and did all of their own trading at Charles Schwab ever since.

He also told me they were finally ready to hire a financial advisor who could help protect them from estate taxes and create their ideal lifetime income stream using the least amount of their assets, as passing on a legacy to their children and some of their charities was incredibly important to them.

Finally, they hit me with it.

Mr. Smith revealed to me that they had well over $18 million in their estate and that pretty much all of it was liquid. And because they were with Schwab for so long, they didn't even have a trust set up. It was all just sitting there in a couple of different accounts at Schwab. The only thing that they set up was a living will.

Not only that, but after spending the past hour and a half telling me about their lives, they both verbally agreed that they felt that, based on everything they had seen and heard, their guts were telling them I was the guy to get them through retirement.

Let me tell you, if I wasn't sitting down, I think my legs might have buckled on me. In all of my years of financial planning, I dreamed of a client like this. This was like hitting a home run in the ninth inning of the World Series to win the game. This was like winning a gold medal in the Olympics or scoring the winning shot in the World Cup. And it was happening to me!

The only somewhat bad news came when they mentioned that before they ever made any financial move, they always consulted their CPA, who was the only person they ever trusted to watch over their money and monitor what they did with it.

Oh great, I thought. *The same CPA who is such a financial planning expert, yet didn't even think to tell you to set up a trust...*

I wasn't about to let that or anything else get in my way or discourage me. This was exactly the kind of good fortune I needed after losing the radio show.

The irony was that if I brought on a client like this, I wouldn't even care about the radio show, and I could finally build out a robust marketing platform without any fear of having to see a new client from the investment immediately.

I was smart enough to realize that my burning love for instant gratification had really been my Achilles' heel over the past decade. With any and all money that I invested into marketing, I usually never had the patience or bankroll to pay for anything except instant and immediate results. But that was all going to change!

I was so excited that I couldn't wait to get home and tell Jen. Things were finally going to be different. This was the catalyst I needed and had been praying for all of these years.

Of course, I did my very best to hide my excitement in front of the Smiths, and they stayed around and chatted with me for another 20 minutes before we all agreed that they would come back in one week with all of their statements, so we could start coming up with some solutions.

And the best part was that I truly knew I could help this couple with their retirement. Gosh, just opening a trust for them to protect their assets and making sure their selected beneficiaries were protected would be a huge improvement in itself. And I couldn't wait to show them some other safe alternatives I was thinking up as well.

That meeting made up for all of the negative things that happened over the past week. I was so excited, I was tempted to cancel all of my afternoon appointments and surprise Jen. However, Judy reminded me that I had two of my best clients coming in who absolutely hated to even be left in the lobby, let alone be canceled on.

"Not to mention that these new prospects with the money haven't signed anything yet, Steve. And you know that the big ones are always the hardest to finally bring on and move their money. So don't go forgetting about your current clients just yet," said Judy.

She was right about not forgetting my current clients. And she was even more right about the big-dollar prospects being the toughest to get a final commitment to move all of their assets. But

I had yet to see one with this kind of money all sitting at Schwab with no broker trying to conserve and defend it. I pinched myself one last time to make sure I wasn't dreaming.

Island Time

As I was driving home that evening, I couldn't stop thinking about the Smiths. Perhaps the radio show getting canceled happened because of some bigger picture? I would have never imagined that I would be hand-delivered a prospect like this on the exact same day I was canceling my radio show.

And just think, once I bring these clients on board and overwhelm them with help, support, and love, they certainly must have other close friends who are wealthy and have been investing on their own also, I thought. I had yet to find a rich couple who only hung around with poor people. The old saying that your income is the average of the five closest people around you seemed to be true more often than not.

While I was pulling into the driveway about a good hour earlier than I usually did, I looked down to see my cell phone ringing. It was Jen. *Probably wondering if I can pick up something on my way home later tonight,* I thought. I let it ring while I hurried to the door to surprise her with my exciting news.

As I bolted through the front door, my wife was in the kitchen and gave me a warm but definitely surprised look.

"Well, to what do we owe the honor of having you home at a decent hour on a Monday? Did you quit your job or something?" Jen asked with a smile. "I was actually just trying to call you about picking up some vegetables at the store on your way home, but I'll gladly take you home early over vegetables any day," she said, before leaning in to kiss me on the lips.

"Babe, you won't believe what happened today," I said enthusiastically. "I had the dream clients come in to meet me for the first time after they saw me present at last Thursday's seminar. They are an incredibly nice couple, both shy of 70 years old; they have over $18 million in assets, and they don't even have a broker. They have been doing all of their trading at Schwab, and they finally realized that they need a real plan to get their retirement assets protected and create a legacy for their children."

"Well, are you sure that they want to invest with you?" asked a somewhat skeptical Jen. "I recall all too many prospects that had you moaning after coming in to see you, just to kick the tires while using you to get information to take back to their broker or family member who was in the industry."

"Keep in mind that this couple doesn't have a broker," I replied in a matter-of-fact tone. "In fact, the last broker or financial advisor they had was over a decade ago, and they fired him. Not to mention, these people actually both verbally agreed in my office that they wanted to move forward with me. They have been to quite a few seminars like mine and were waiting to find someone they wanted to partner up with on their retirement journey. And they said that person is me!

"And Jen, don't think for a minute that I am going to let this one slip out of my hands. My entire focus for the next few weeks will be bending over backward to make sure that they are happy, that I can give them the best advice to fit their needs, and that I make it a complete no-brainer for them to move forward with me," I said confidently.

"I am really proud of you, Steve," said Jen. "All of your hard work is starting to pay off, and the kids and I are rooting for you more than anyone because your success means we will get to see you more often."

"Do you know what I was thinking on the drive home tonight?" I asked her.

She stared at me, wondering what I could possibly say next.

"I was thinking that it is finally time to book that trip to the Caribbean you have always been wanting to do. Just you and me… no kids. What do you think?" I asked with a big smile.

She stumbled for words, "I… I… well… are you serious, Steve? And do you think we should book it before you even close this new client? I don't want to say no to a trip that I have been dying to go on for the last six years, but I also recall just this past weekend you saying that we would have to start making some financial cutbacks. Are you sure that you are ready to book it already? Because once we book the trip, I am going with or without you," Jen said with a slight smile.

"Yes, let's book it tonight. Our dinner conversation this past weekend reminded me just how bad of a husband I have been. My job has consumed me, and it is time that I start making up for it. Besides, these new prospects will be clients soon. Even if I just get to handle a portion of their money until they get 100 percent comfortable, it will be a huge windfall for me. But I can't think of anything that could derail this deal."

7

MOMENT OF TRUTH

The trip to the Caribbean was booked, and Jen and I would be headed to the island of St. John in a few months. Personally, I was pretty excited to take this much-needed and well-deserved trip with my wife.

When I made it to the office, Judy let me know that I had received the official termination paperwork from the radio station, along with a brief, but nice note from vice president and soon-to-be-unemployed Drew, wishing me the best of luck.

It was a bittersweet ending to my radio show, as I was going to miss the credibility and steady flow of leads that came from my show each week. What I wasn't going to miss were the "might as well be yacht payments" and the treks to and from the radio studio to do my recordings.

Not to mention, just finding enough interesting content to talk about each week was a job in itself sometimes. There were only so many ways to say the same thing about financial prosperity over and over again!

This week was an important one, seeing that the Smiths were coming in for their second appointment, when they would bring in all of their statements from Schwab, along with any other assets to discuss.

During our last meeting, we agreed that when they came back in, they would bring all of their statements; we would discuss a thorough plan; and then they would go home and think about everything, do any necessary research, and decide to either move forward with all, some, or none of my recommendations the following week.

I structured my prospect appointments into a three-step agenda after hearing the success of one of my mentors. There was an optional fourth appointment, if needed, but I found that I could close well using the three-appointment process.

The first meeting was all about meeting each other, finding out if the prospect had pain, and then seeing if we were compatible with each other. If not, we parted ways as friends. If we both liked each other, I asked the prospect to come again one week from that day and to bring all of their statements and be prepared to talk about a retirement plan. I also let them know that even if they loved what I recommended, I didn't allow anyone to invest or make a final decision until the third, or even sometimes the fourth, appointment. No exceptions.

By setting the agenda up front, I felt it set them at ease, and it broke down any barriers of them thinking they were going to get "sold" on the next meeting. It also made them trust me more as an advisor who really wanted to do the best thing for them as opposed to a product slinger who wanted to aggressively close on the first meeting.

When the prospect came in for the second meeting, we uncovered and went over all of their pains again, all of their frustrations, and then went over each statement as I educated them on what they had, the pros and cons of each of their current investments, and any possible changes that could be made to enhance what they currently had.

At the end of the second meeting, I presented a recommendation of what I thought they should do. I usually had a pretty good idea of where I was going with each client as early as the first appointment, since they always revealed what kind of money they had and where it was currently held.

I used the statements as verification and then presented an overall plan that was usually thought out and ready to show before they even arrived for the second time.

Occasionally, I had to change an annuity product or life insurance product, depending on new things brought to the table during the meeting, but as most of the money that I took control of was going into managed money, I could easily spit out illustrations and portfolio hypotheticals right there on my computer in front of them. Most prospects seemed to be impressed that I could do all of it right in front of them as I kept it all up on a 52-inch LCD screen on the wall.

Another important thing I always did at the close of the second meeting was get them to tell me "yes" or "no" before they left.

For instance, at the end of the meeting, I would ask the prospects something like this, "Assuming that my recommendations can solve all of the problems that you have, can you think of any reasons that you wouldn't move forward with my recommended plans?" (It was important to reiterate their pain points.)

I let them know that I only accepted "yes" or "no" answers. "Maybe," "perhaps," and "I need to think about it" were not accepted. I would tell them that we were all adults, and it was fair to both of us if they would either say, "Yes, this makes sense" or "No, I am still not comfortable."

Almost everyone said "yes," and once this happened, I rarely lost a case or failed to convert a prospect to a client. I noticed that most people inherently wanted to stay consistent with what they said, so once they agreed, it was painful for them to be inconsistent.

Finally, once they agreed to move forward (assuming I could solve their problems), I set the agenda for the third and final meeting. I let them know that this next meeting was always held four business days from the second meeting, and that in this final meeting, we would sign the paperwork to start moving money and agree to enter into a formal relationship, where I would take the reins to get them through the rest of their life.

I told them that over the next four days, they were encouraged to do any research and call me with any clarifications or questions. Once they showed up on the third appointment, I expected them to be ready to go with signing paperwork and starting the movement of money.

Finally, we would set them up with a secure username and password so that they could log in to our client portal any time and see how their entire portfolio was doing. Then, we'd send them off feeling great, and Judy would start the bird-dogging of making sure all transfers and requests to move accounts happened as quickly as possible. We would also send a new update on all money transfers every Friday, so they always knew exactly where their investments stood.

The Second Meeting

The Smiths sent me an email the day before our meeting, confirming they would be there, and they also reminded me that they would be bringing along their trusted CPA. According to their email, because this was the first time in well over a decade they had ever considered going back with a broker, they wanted a third party whom they trusted to be there.

Past prospects brought in their CPAs, kids, attorneys, and one even brought in her priest, so I had no issue with this. In fact, I actually preferred it, as I knew that I could be more persuasive face-to-face with their CPA than they ever could when trying to regurgitate our conversations to him.

I also knew that if I could convince the CPA that this was a great deal for the Smiths, then the deal was done. And since they did all of their own trading and clearly had not thought about important issues like putting a trust in place, I knew that if I couldn't improve their position, I didn't deserve the business.

The appointment with the Smiths was scheduled at 11 o'clock in the morning. I looked down at my watch and realized I was one hour away from go time. I normally didn't get anxious or spend too much time overanalyzing my recommendations, but this meeting was a little bit different than the average prospect that walked into my office.

I entered the reception area, where Judy had a large U-shaped desk, and I saw her fidgeting around in an odd fashion, almost as though she was nervous.

Trying not to startle her, I said in a mild manner, "Hey, Judy, how you feeling?"

"Oh my gosh, you scared me, Steve. I didn't know you were here. I guess I was so preoccupied, thinking about your big meeting today," she said.

"Now, why in the world would you be thinking and worrying about this meeting? I am the one who should be the nervous wreck," I said jokingly.

Judy looked up at me with some concern and said, "Steve, when I received the call from the radio station last week, I knew that it was going to hit your business pretty hard. And over the past couple of months, I could tell you were under a lot of stress. I never wanted to say anything because, quite frankly, it isn't any of my business. But my main worry was that if things got any slower, you would have to get rid of me or sell the company or something. I really enjoy this job, and I guess sometimes I feel just as anxious as you because I know that my job depends on you closing big accounts like this... I hope that makes sense."

"Of course, Judy," I assured her. "Don't ever worry for a minute about your job security. With or without this large prospect becoming a client, you have a job with me for as long as you want it. In fact, I don't know what I would do without you."

"Thanks, Steve," she said with a big smile. "That means a lot."

"Listen, I am going to head back and do one final review of everything that I want to go over with them. Give me a quick heads up when they pull up, make sure all of the lights are on, and let's turn the air conditioner down just a bit to make it inviting and comfortable," I said.

"I'm on it. Best of luck today," Judy said.

Showtime

It was 10 minutes until our appointment time, and Judy buzzed my line to let me know that a car pulled up. However, she told me it wasn't the same car they came in last time; it appeared to be a man by himself—and it certainly wasn't Mr. Smith.

I let Judy know that it was probably the CPA who was going to join the Smiths. "Let me know when all three of them are here, and don't send them all back until everyone is present," I said.

I quickly checked the mirror in my office to make sure I didn't have anything in my teeth, said a quick prayer, and then sat down and waited for show time.

Just 30 seconds later, Judy buzzed in to let me know that all three of them were walking up to the door.

"Send 'em through, Judy," I replied.

"Will do, Steve. Knock 'em dead," she answered.

As the Smiths came in, followed by their CPA friend whom they introduced as Craig, I asked them to take a seat and then asked if they had any pressing questions since our last meeting that I could address before we had some fun.

They both looked at each other and said that they still had a good feeling about me as an advisor and what I could do for them. They were excited to review all of their current investments and see what recommendations I could make to improve things.

I looked at their CPA friend to see if he had any concerns, and he gave me a professional smile and said he was excited to see what I had in mind as well.

"Perfect," I said. "Well then, let's get started by going over every investment statement that you have so I can get a better idea of where everything is. Just like a doctor who needs to know all of your pains, your past issues, and your medications before making a diagnosis, I work in the same way, in that I simply can't even begin to talk about solutions until I know all of the facts. Do you have all of your statements ready?"

As they handed them over, I was not only impressed with the massive size of the folder, but I was also amazed at how well they organized everything. I could see that they had different folders for each account at Schwab and even had many of the individual statements broken down by quarter, along with all notifications of stock splits, fee statements, and so on.

It was refreshing to work with wealthy people, and it was also refreshing to work with well-organized people. I couldn't tell you how many prospects and clients came in missing pages to their statements, or even worse, had no idea where their statements or copies of their policies were.

The next thing I knew, I glanced over at the clock on my wall and noticed that the meeting had already hit the two-hour mark.

Not only did they have a plethora of different investments at Schwab, they also had questions about almost every single investment except for their money market account. It appeared as if they did all of their own research on these investments over the years, and this was the very first time they were getting a second opinion and speaking to a financial professional about their decisions.

In some investments they did quite well, but in others, they lost a significant amount of money by being too aggressive, following the "dumb money," and simply by letting their emotions run some of their trading.

As we went through and discussed each statement and investment of theirs, I took detailed notes of the pros and cons of each one along with my suggested plan of attack. I was careful to always include the Smiths and their CPA on each recommended change to make sure they were comfortable, answer any questions, and then get them to agree that it made sense to make the change before I wrote it down on my pad.

In some cases, we all agreed that it made sense to make no changes, and I documented those on the pad.

Throughout the two-hour statement overview, I became more and more impressed with the Smiths. It was clear they were incredibly smart people who understood the power of investing, and they knew exactly what they wanted and didn't want. And when they saw an investment that they wanted and believed made sense for them, they jumped on it without a second thought.

It made me feel even better that they selected me as their "go-to" advisor for the "second half" of their life, and I could only hope they jumped in head first with full trust in my services and recommendations like they had with their past investments.

Their CPA friend stayed quiet throughout the questions and answers, but always made sure to chime in with tax questions whenever I mentioned potentially selling certain investments. I believed he was impressed with my answers, as I prided myself on knowing more about taxable investment events than any of my competitors.

After the last statement was thoroughly covered, I looked up at the Smiths and congratulated them for the incredible job they did managing their own money for the past decade, especially considering the two huge market corrections and wild volatility we all lived through. Certainly they fared better than many of the money managers I competed with.

"Well, we made it through without any tears or fistfights," I said with a laugh. "Now that we have discussed all of your investments, let's take a quick 10-minute break before we review my notes on all of the recommended changes."

"Sounds great," piped Mr. Smith.

After our much-needed bathroom and coffee break, we were all back in my office to go over the new plan.

I went through each recommended change, including adding in some annuities, a new universal life insurance policy for both of them, and some tactical asset strategies that I would use to manage the largest chunk of their money.

Most of the questioning came from Craig, the CPA, who needed further clarification to protect his clients from large taxable events.

The Smiths continued to nod, made comments about how much it all made sense, and agreed with my recommendations. The meeting was like a dream come true.

After another 30 minutes went by, we were on my very last recommendation. I asked the Smiths how they felt about all of the proposed changes and if they had any concerns.

The two of them looked at each other and then at me, as Mrs. Smith said, "Steve, this looks great. We are really excited to have a trusted advisor like you on our side."

"Thank you both. And thank you as well, Craig, for coming along and adding some very important feedback to this meeting," I said.

Now, it was time for the second meeting close, where expectations were set for the third and final meeting.

"Do you both agree that my recommendations have answered and solved all of the objections that you came in with?" I asked.

The both nodded in agreement.

"Do you both agree that my recommendations are clear, make sense for you financially, and put you in a better overall retirement position?" I asked.

"Absolutely," said Mr. Smith.

"And I assume you would let me know right now if you had any reason or doubt to not move forward with the plan I have described and outlined for you?"

"Correct. We feel very good about everything, Steve," said Mrs. Smith.

"I am glad to hear that," I responded back. "If you don't mind, I will bring Judy in to get all of your information so she can start filling in most of the paperwork. That way, when you come back for the next appointment, you won't have anything to fill out except your signatures."

"Sounds great. We are ready," said Mr. Smith.

As Judy came in to get down all of their information and made copies of their driver's licenses and all of their statements, I reassured the Smiths that none of their holdings or money would move until the next meeting when they signed the final paperwork.

I also reminded them that if they had any questions, thoughts, or concerns over the next few days, they should never hesitate to call me at any time. The next few days would be their opportunity to digest it all, do any research on my recommendations, and iron out any last-minute changes.

We adjourned the meeting by agreeing that the Smiths would come back in to the office in four days to sign all of the final forms and paperwork and start moving money.

It was one of my longest meetings in a while. But boy, was it a great one.

Yes, it was a great day indeed.

8

RADIO SILENCE

After saying goodbye to the Smiths and Craig, I briefly met with Judy to make sure she had everything she needed and gave her some final instructions regarding which applications and forms to start filling out.

I also wrote up a quick thank you note to the Smiths on my nice stationary and had Judy send that off in the afternoon mail. I wasn't going to miss out on any chance to "wow" this couple.

Now, it was time to head home to share the exciting news with Jen and the kids. *Perhaps we will all go out to dinner together*, I thought. Sadly, I couldn't recall the last time we did that as a family.

I arrived at my front door, grinning from ear to ear and very anxious to share the news.

Jen saw me immediately and rushed over to say, "How did it go, honey?"

"It could not have gone any better. We spent almost four hours together, and they verbally agreed to move forward with approximately $14 million. A few of their holdings weren't as liquid as we thought, but I am getting everything else. All they have to do is come back in a few days and sign the paperwork. I can't tell you how big this is, Jen!" I exclaimed.

"Steve, that is incredible! I am so happy for you, and I know that you deserve this more than anyone," Jen said.

"What do you say we get the kids together and go have a celebratory dinner tonight?" I suggested. "It has been way too long."

"Let's do it. I will go round up the kids and let them know. They will be so happy to hear that you are taking us out like old times," she said.

Back at the Office

"Did you ever hear back from the Smiths about the question you had on one of their statements?" I asked Judy.

"Not a word. Do you want me to call them again?" replied Judy.

"Yes, since tomorrow is the final appointment, go ahead and call again. If you get their voicemail, just tell them that we're calling as a courtesy reminder for their third appointment tomorrow at 11 a.m. That way, they don't think we are harassing them," I said.

"Will do, Steve. I will keep you posted on how it goes," she said.

I went back to my desk, hoping nothing had gone wrong with the Smiths in the last couple of days. It wasn't like them to not return calls. But perhaps they were out and about. I knew they had some kids around Florida, and it could be they made a short trip out of it.

Judy poked her head in. "No one picked up at the Smith residence, so I called his cell phone. No answer there, so I left a courtesy reminder about tomorrow's meeting."

"Thanks, Judy." I couldn't help but wonder if something was wrong. Having a hot prospect—especially the biggest one of your career—go silent is a salesman's worst nightmare. And this was usually the time when my mind started running through all kinds of scenarios. However, I wasn't going to let it get the best of me.

I knew the best thing to do in these kinds of situations was go blow off steam, get any negative thoughts out of my head, and get out of the office. I checked my calendar, and noticed I didn't have another appointment for three hours.

Time to go hit some golf balls at the driving range.

As I blasted golf balls out around the 250-yard marker with my driver, my mind still kept going back to the Smiths. Was something wrong? Did their CPA kill the deal? Were they playing me to get information?

No, I told myself. *There's no way they would have gone to all of that trouble to meet with me for four hours, give me copies of every single one of their statements, give Judy all of their information, including Social Security numbers, and then even verbally agree to move forward if they didn't intend to.*

This reassured me all was fine. "They have every right to not be sitting by the phone waiting for my call," I said to myself. "It wasn't like we told them that we were going to be calling that day. I am blowing this entire thing way out of proportion."

At any rate, I was out of balls to hit, so it was time to head back to the office for my afternoon meeting.

My 3 o'clock clients showed up for their annual review, and I hated to admit it, but I really had trouble staying focused. All

I could think about were the Smiths. After reviewing these clients' modest gains in their portfolio and making just one small recommendation that they move some money out of bonds and back into equities, I waved goodbye to them and wished them the best

Once they were clear of the office, I turned to Judy and asked her if she ever heard anything back from either Mr. or Mrs. Smith.

"Not a peep," Judy said. "Should I email them?"

"No, let's not get too far ahead of ourselves. They are coming in tomorrow at 11 a.m., so no need to pester them. And even though they might be a bit older, I am guessing that they have caller ID, and we don't want to look desperate," I said.

After going back to my office to return emails, I looked up and noticed that it was already 5:30. My wife was in such a good mood over the last week with me coming home at a decent hour, so I figured, why not keep putting a big smile on her face? Not to mention it wasn't going to do me any good to sit around the office and daydream about the next day's final appointment.

"See you tomorrow, Judy," I said as I hustled out the door.

"I'm right behind you Steve," she said. "Get some sleep—tomorrow is the big day."

"That's right. It's going to be our biggest day yet," I exclaimed.

But something was still bothering me about the Smiths, even though I kept reminding myself how sold they were on moving forward with me.

The Third Appointment

It was the big day, and I woke up energized and ready to make history at Kennedy Financial.

I left the house early, well before the kids or Jen were up. And I couldn't wait to come home that evening and celebrate with my two awesome kids and supportive wife.

When I arrived at the office, I was pleasantly surprised to see Judy already there. I occasionally wondered if she actually slept there some nights. *When all of the money is officially moved over from this large client, I am going to do something really nice for Judy. She really is the glue that holds this business together many weeks.*

I greeted Judy with a big smile and then hesitantly asked her if she heard anything back from the Smiths the night before.

"Nothing, yet. I can only imagine that they will just wait to see you today versus calling last night," Judy said.

It was actually good news they didn't call the previous night; I couldn't tell you how many times we arrived in the morning to get a late-night voicemail from a client canceling on us.

These late-night callers clearly thought we would get mad or try to sell them on not canceling if they had to speak to us, so they purposely called well after hours to leave us their cancellation notice on the voicemail. Some of the excuses we heard sounded like a sixth-grader saying his or her homework was eaten by the dog.

I fired up my computer, answered my emails, put in a few early trade orders, and tried my best to occupy the time before the Smiths arrived. I had purposely blocked off the entire day, and my hope was that this would be a quick meeting of signing paperwork followed by me heading home to pop open a bottle of champagne with Jen.

Finally, it was only 20 minutes until 11 o'clock, and surprisingly, I was completely calm.

This third appointment really wasn't all that stressful. It was the second appointment that was the toughest, as getting someone who barely knows you to agree to move their money out of where they currently have it and into your recommendations is not as easy as it sounds.

In a sense, you were telling the prospects that their money was not working for them correctly, they had been missing out on better opportunities, and their planning was inferior to yours.

It was a weird dynamic, because some people were incredibly grateful that you showed them a better path. Others, though, were a bit hostile and defended their brokers or themselves (if they managed their money like the Smiths).

Fortunately for me, the Smiths were nothing but appreciative, as the wealthy usually understood the significance of someone showing them a better way to do things, especially when it came down to making them more money.

Speaking of the Smiths, where were they?

I buzzed Judy's desk.

"Hey, Steve," Judy said. "No sign of them yet. Shall I call them?"

"Well, it is only two minutes past. Let's give them until 10 minutes after and then call," I said.

I sank back into my chair and stared up at the clock. Could it be that the Smiths had a change of heart? But even so, why would they not have at least called? Perhaps their CPA didn't say much while he was here and then threw me under the bus when they left. Maybe they were out there shopping me around.

All kinds of negative thoughts went through my head as the time ticked away. And then, all of a sudden, I could hear the phone ring at Judy's desk. I peeked through the door to see Judy's reaction.

"Sure," Judy said. "Let me get Steve on the phone."

Judy placed the call on hold and turned to me to let me know that it was the Smiths and that they needed to talk to me.

My heartbeat and anxiety went through the roof! Were they calling to tell me that their car broke down or that they had a family emergency? Or were they calling to cancel the entire deal? I could feel small beads of sweat forming on my forehead as I sat back down, took a deep breath, and picked up the phone receiver.

"Hey, Mr. and Mrs. Smith, it is Steve here," I said, not exactly sure what to lead with.

Mr. Smith spoke first. "Hey, Steve. We sincerely apologize that we are late today."

OK, so maybe it isn't as bad as I thought. Perhaps they are just calling to apologize for running late and they are on their way, I thought to myself.

Mr. Smith went on calmly, "We have appreciated your candidness and honesty since the day we met you, and we feel that it is only right to be completely transparent with you on where Debbie and I are with all of this."

I felt my stomach knot up. The sweat beads were coming at a rapid speed on my forehead. My heart was racing. I could sense that they were about to tell me about their second thoughts or even a complete change of heart.

Mr. Smith continued talking, "The reason we are late is that we need a little more time. Debbie and I debated about coming in today, and we were actually on the way, but turned around when we both agreed it wasn't fair to you or us if we showed up not 100 percent ready," he explained. "We didn't have our cell phone in the car, otherwise we would have called before 11 so you didn't think we were bailing on you."

That would have been nice! And what are they trying to say here anyway? I thought.

He seemed to pause, so I interjected, "So, is there something in particular that you aren't comfortable with or that I can answer to make you feel at ease?"

There was a brief silence on the other end. I could sense that the couple was probably in the same room looking at each other, wondering who was going to deliver me the bad news.

Larry Smith finally spoke again. "Steve, we really like you; we trust that you have built a very solid retirement plan, but we just aren't completely ready to move forward without some further research.

"We don't have cold feet, we just need some more time to research your recommendations online. Keep in mind that we have been doing our own research and investing for over 10 years now, so a change of the guard on our entire nest egg isn't as easy for us to digest as we thought it would be. And we are talking about a lot of hard-earned money here," Larry explained.

Time to do my best to save this by being the nice guy instead of a pushy salesman.

"Larry and Debbie, I really do understand your situation, and I really appreciate your honesty. The last thing I want you to do is move forward with something that you aren't excited and satisfied with," I said.

"Thanks for understanding," said Debbie. "We just need a couple more days to do some Internet research, and then we will be ready to make a decision."

"I understand, and I encourage you to do as much Internet research as you need. But before I let you go, are you are sure that there isn't anything in particular bothering you or that I can address now?" I asked one final time, hoping to get some sort of inclination of an underlying problem.

"There is nothing in particular except a couple more days to get completely comfortable," said Mr. Smith.

Time to take control of the conversation and set the agenda, I thought.

"OK. Well, today is Tuesday. Do you think you will have a decision by Thursday or Friday?" I asked.

"How about we agree to meet or talk again on Friday morning? That will give us plenty of time to do research, digest it all, and then sleep on it for a few nights," said Larry.

"Fair enough. Let's count on Friday morning at the same time," I said.

"See you then, Steve. And thank you for understanding," said Debbie.

As I slowly hung up the receiver, all I could think was: *Where did I go wrong? What could I have done differently to ensure they didn't get cold feet? Was I too lazy in my assumption that this would be easy for them to grasp and adapt to? Should I have stretched it out to the fourth appointment?*

Something just didn't feel right, and I had a bad sense that they weren't telling me everything. I dealt with way too many clients in my career to know that there was usually an underlying fear or issue that was holding them back from moving forward. The tough part was peeling back the layers to find out the main issue.

I couldn't afford to let this one slip through my fingers, and I was going to do whatever it took to get the Smiths comfortable.

Then, I had to go face reality and tell an anxious Judy and hopeful Jen that the deal wasn't going to happen yet. It was a crummy Tuesday.

9

THE ANSWER

Jen handled the news better than I did, presumably because she was previously witness to countless deals getting postponed due to a myriad of different reasons. She believed that at the end of the day, if the deal was meant to happen, it would happen.

In the meantime, I couldn't sleep the rest of the week, as my head continued to come up with every possible best- and worst-case scenario that I could dream up. And even in the office, my mind was wandering aimlessly. I wasn't the same Steve I usually was, and I was sure that both Judy and my Wednesday and Thursday clients could sense something was off.

I made it through the week, and even though I barely slept a lick the night before, I still felt good Friday morning. After a quick shower and a cup of joe, I was ready to face the big day ahead of me.

Since our chat on Tuesday, I had not heard a word from the Smiths. I was tempted to reach out more than once to see if I could find their source of doubt, but I knew that any attempt to contact them would make me look insecure and desperate.

As I pulled up to the office that beautiful Friday morning, I knew the day would be one that I wouldn't forget, for better or worse.

Even though my mind conjured up all kinds of negative scenarios (and even a few conspiracy theories) as to why they would not move forward, I was still convinced they would become clients.

I answered all of their objections, solved their problems, and put them in a significantly better position for their remaining years on Earth. Even their CPA seemed satisfied with my recommendations, and convincing a CPA wasn't an easy task!

It was 15 minutes until 11 o'clock, and my mind began to wander again. Would they show up at all? Would they call like they did last time to tell me they still hadn't decided? Or would they walk in here and sign all of the paperwork like nothing happened?

I was counting down the minutes and trying to do anything I could to speed up the time and get my mind off of this big, upcoming moment. I had already read and reread my recent emails. I spoke to Judy until it became clear we had nothing else to talk about. *Just hurry up and get here, 11:00 a.m.!*

A few minutes passed, when Judy buzzed me and excitedly said, "Steve, they just pulled up. And they are quite a few minutes early. Shall I send them through?"

"Absolutely," I said. Even if I wanted to pretend to be busy and have them wait until their scheduled 11 o'clock appointment, I couldn't stand the suspense myself.

Their early arrival had to be a good sign, I thought. If they were dreading telling me bad news, why would they come early?

Judy opened my office door and led Mr. and Mrs. Smith to sit down in the two big brown leather chairs that faced my desk.

"Great to see both of you," I said with a big smile. "I hope you were able to do some research and come to a conclusion over the past couple of days."

I tried to get a sense of what they were thinking by their facial expressions, but both Larry and Debbie kept perfect poker faces.

"Yes, Steve. Thank you again for giving us some extra time. This is a really big decision that not only affects us, but also impacts our next two generations as well," said Debbie.

"I completely understand," I said.

"Well, since we both know that you didn't come here for small talk or Judy's coffee, let's just address the elephant in the room and get down to what you are thinking about all of this. Have you made a final decision on how you would like to proceed?" I asked.

There was a brief, awkward silence as the two of them looked at each other as if to mentally ask who was going to spill the news.

After what seemed like an eternity, Mr. Smith finally said, "Steve, this entire decision has been incredibly tough for us. We came to your dinner workshop completely skeptical. However, you won us over very quickly when you gave us free advice that not even our well-paid old broker attempted to do. Moreover, we felt as if you were a man of integrity and that you enjoyed helping your clients."

Larry continued, "The one thing that is incredibly important to us is that we have just one expert who gets us through the rest of our lives. We don't want to settle for second best, and we certainly don't want to change financial advisors in the middle of our retirement years."

I sat there nodding at his words, still wondering which way he was going with all of this.

Larry briefly glanced at Debbie and then went on, "I was raised by my parents to always be transparent, and then my stint in the Navy engrained in me the importance of addressing issues face to face, regardless of how uncomfortable they were. And that brings us to why we are here today."

My stomach was beginning to tighten, and I began to feel the same way I felt when my first love in college sat me down to break up with me, starting off with the fluff before she laid down the breakup hammer.

Larry went on to say, "Steve, we truly do like you, believe in most of your recommendations, and believe that you have done your best to put us in a better position financially."

I looked them both in the eyes and simply nodded yes.

"And whether wrong or right, we believe that we are not a normal client for most financial advisors due to our large net worth. That being said, both Debbie and I agree that we only want to work with the absolute best financial expert who specializes in high-net-worth clientele," he said and then paused.

Not knowing exactly what to say, I calmly said, "I agree with you that you are certainly not the normal client for any financial advisor. But I hope that you understand that not only am I qualified to work with high-net-worth clients, I have many millionaire clients whom I have serviced happily for almost a decade now."

There was more awkward silence, and then Larry spoke up again after glancing quickly at Debbie to see if she was going to offer anything.

"Steve, when we came home that evening after our first appointment with you, we were truly excited. We believed that we finally found a great fit with an expert advisor who could protect our finances for the rest of our lives."

I was beginning to wonder where in the world this conversation was going.

Larry continued, "And after the second meeting, we came home even more excited as the ideas and recommendations that you presented really made a ton of sense for us. Gosh, even our CPA agreed that everything you recommended was very sound. But even in all of the excitement, we still wanted to spend some serious time checking out the annuity product you recommended, the two life insurance products, and all of the tactical managed money recommendations as well. And finally, we wanted to do some research on you, too."

"And to be very frank with you, Steve, that is where the problems arose," Larry said. "When we started doing research on you and Kennedy Financial Services, we didn't find much of anything. There was a partially completed LinkedIn profile that looked like you didn't put much effort into it, there was a link about you winning some award for being a top salesman for some insurance marketing company, and then there was a link to some site that talked about a client complaint on you from a few years back."

I interjected, "I can explain that client complaint, and please believe me that this is not something that I am trying to hide. In fact, it is public knowledge that the complaint was eventually dismissed with no wrongdoing on my end, and I am quite proud that I was able to prove my innocence in the deal."

"Yes," said Mrs. Smith. "We did read that you were acquitted of a false claim that appeared to be just an angry client trying to throw you under the bus. But that wasn't the real problem."

"Well, what was it?" I asked.

Mr. Smith looked me and said, "Steve, we just couldn't find anything about you online. This might not seem important to you, but for people like Debbie and me, who are only willing to invest our money with the very best financial advisor, it is tough to believe that an expert doesn't have a website. I mean, can you name a single professional who doesn't? We've found other advisors with websites, articles, blogs, videos, and reviews from the people or companies they helped. But we couldn't find anything about you.

I felt as if the room was spinning. I heard just about every excuse out there, but not only was this one new to me, I didn't know how to respond.

I could say that my RIA designation held me back from being online, or that I didn't think most of my clients were online searching for financial advice, so I didn't spend much time building up my reputation, or I could just tell them the truth: I had never even considered it important to be on the web until right now.

Larry kept going, "Steve, I am guessing that you don't agree with this thinking, but at the end of the day, we decided we could never consider giving our entire life savings to a so-called 'expert' who couldn't be found online, never mind one who didn't even take the time to fill out his LinkedIn. Why would our financial plan be treated any differently?"

I was stunned. I was about to lose the biggest prospect of my entire career over a stupid half-filled-out LinkedIn page and an old complaint I resolved years ago. This just didn't make any sense.

"Listen, Steve," Larry continued to say. "I know you don't like hearing this, and Debbie and I really hated that we had to come in today and tell you the bad news. I hate the fact that we took so much of your time, especially after we verbally agreed to move forward last week. I am sure that it probably got you incredibly excited to have us as a new client, and now we changed everything."

That's an understatement, I thought to myself.

"However, when we told you we'd work with you, it was contingent on the fact that we could research both you and your recommendations, but we just kept coming to the same conclusion: You are not the expert we need to help us prepare for the coming years. I know this might sound cliché, but it's purely a business decision," Larry said. "And after a considerable discussion with my wife, and even quite a bit of prayer, our guts keep telling us that you are not the perfect fit."

As he continued to speak, I went numb. "If we could give you any advice on helping people like us, it would be for you to present yourself as the financial expert in Orlando. I can assure you that all of our friends do the exact same kind of research. We all talk about the seminars we've been to whenever we're together. And the one thing we all agree on is that we want to work with an expert. How can you expect us to trust you with our money if we can't find any information about you?" Larry added as a final slap in the face.

Larry appeared to be finished talking, and the room became so quiet you could've heard a feather drop. They both looked up at me, probably wondering if I was about to cry, scream and shout, or throw something. Quite honestly, I felt paralyzed.

Out of all the scenarios I played out in my head, both positive and negative, nothing like this had ever crossed my mind. I hoped a hidden camera crew would bust in the door, laughing at the joke they pulled on me, but the longer I let this sink in, the more I realized this wasn't a joke or a dream.

I asked the Smiths the first of two questions that came to mind, hoping I'd find any chance of conserving them as clients.

"I really appreciate your honesty, and I admire the fact that you came down here to do this in person. Most people wouldn't do that.

"You are correct, although I don't completely agree that having a website could make or break the deal. I do, however, understand your concerns," I said, as reserved as I could.

I continued, "Please tell me, is there anything that I can say or do to change your minds? I have worked incredibly hard since we met to solve your problems, and we all agreed that my recommendations could get you to a much better financial position than you were in before. Please tell me there is something that I can do to prove I can be the expert that you are looking for."

The room once again fell deathly silent as the Smiths both looked at each other to see who was going to answer this loaded question.

My silence continued while I smiled at them and prayed for one last shot, when Mrs. Smith finally chimed in, "Steve, we are truly sorry, but there is nothing that can change our minds at this point. As you may be able to tell, we make up our minds pretty quickly, and we usually stick with it, even if that makes us look. It has served us well for many years."

I couldn't argue with that, but it certainly didn't help the nauseous feeling in my stomach.

I had to know one more thing before they left my office, so I went out on a limb and asked, "Can you at least be candid with me? Have you found another financial advisor, or are you just going to keep your investments at Schwab for now?"

There was a little more awkward silence, as they glanced at each other.

Finally, Larry said, "Steve, I know that you don't want to hear this, but you did ask, and I was always taught to be honest... the answer is, while we were researching your recommendations, we came across a couple of financial advisors who seemed to answer the questions that we were asking.

"One of them had some incredibly in-depth reviews and explanations of the products that we discussed with you, and one of the other advisors online had some of the best videos on retirement planning that we have ever seen, from life insurance, to annuities, to assets under management.

"After we continued to read, we decided to reach out to one of them. Honestly, we felt kind of bad, since it was just a day after meeting with you, but like I said earlier, we believe that we owe it to ourselves to make sure we have the absolute best, and at the end of the day, this is one of the most important decisions we will ever make."

I was almost to the point of a complete breakdown; the severity of what was happening finally hit me. I was not only losing the biggest client to ever walk in my office over a lack of a silly website, but I was losing it to one of these bogus digital financial advisors I despised.

Larry continued, "Although it is too early to make any decisions, we were quite impressed, not only with the one advisor's expertise, but also that he specializes in working with high-net-worth clients like us."

Well, of course he does, I thought. *I bet every advisor who speaks to you would say that.* I decided to take one last stab at it.

"Is this advisor you found online local?" I asked.

"No, he isn't even in Florida," said Larry. "And although we have enjoyed meeting you face to face, it's quite convenient to be able to speak with someone over the phone and via email.

"What most retirees realize pretty quickly is that our time is limited. Our time left is the time that we want to maximize, doing things we enjoy, like traveling, visiting with family, and golfing. And please take no offense, but meeting with financial planners is not high on the list of fun things to do.

"The other nice benefit of dealing with an advisor who is far away from any of our friends or family, is that there is a very little chance of him having a few too many drinks at a cocktail party and slipping up about our net worth, which we like to keep quiet around our friends and neighbors."

I was beginning to wish that I never asked them my second question. I pulled myself back together and tried my best to end this on a positive note.

"Larry and Debbie, it has been a pleasure getting to know you, and I really wish that things had gone differently. I am sick to my stomach, knowing that I am going to lose you to some financial advisor you found online who will most likely take my recommendations and do something very similar.

"But as much as I hate it, sometimes that is just the way the cookie crumbles. I respect your business decision, as it is your hard-earned money we are talking about, not mine. If you ever change your mind or need a second opinion of any kind, all I can ask is that you employ me, as I already have a huge head start by knowing exactly where you stand and what you need. I wish you both the best of luck in retirement," I said, hoping for a miracle that they would somehow change their minds.

However, they promptly stood up, shook my hand, thanked me for all of my time and support, and were out the door.

I stood in my office in complete shock, still a bit confused about exactly what just happened.

10

MORE TROUBLE AHEAD

Two hours after the Smiths left, I was still sitting in my office paralyzed, not really wanting to speak to anyone or do anything.

Judy did her best to console me and get me talking, but I told her that this wasn't a good time and she could take the rest of the day off.

Never in my career had I been so relieved to not have any client or prospect appointments on my calendar. And if there were more appointments that day, I would have had Judy cancel them. I just really wanted to be alone.

My cell phone continued to buzz with both calls and texts, and each time I looked down at it, I saw it was Jen. I figured she was dying to know how my appointment went, and probably already had her favorite rosé champagne ready at the house.

I just didn't have the courage to speak to her yet. What would happen with our trip that we just booked? We couldn't afford it now, and I couldn't afford to be out of the office for a week at this point. What would happen to all of the promises I made her about being around more? And what would I do to replace my radio show that I so quickly dismissed once I thought I was landing this big-fish client?

It was the first time in a while I could remember when I was in my office with no one to see and nothing that needed to get done. At least, I didn't have any ambition to get anything done.

I certainly wasn't going to go home; I wasn't ready to face Jen and the kids yet. And I didn't feel like making any calls or getting on my computer, so I lay down on the waiting room couch and closed my eyes.

I woke up a little disoriented and looked down at my watch. It was 4:30 already, and I still hadn't spoken to Jen. I bet she was freaking out by now.

So I headed back into my office and found my cell phone on my desk. Eight missed calls and seven unread text messages from Jen. She was going to kill me.

I still wasn't ready to head home, but I knew that I had to call Jen to tell her what happened.

"Where in the world have you been?" Jen almost yelled. "I have been worried sick about you and was about to head over to your office before I called the police to find you. What happened today?" she asked.

"Jen, I lost the deal," was all I could muster to say about it.

"Yeah, I already heard the news after calling Judy's cell trying to locate you. Steve, I am really sorry. But please don't let this get in the way of your family. There will be other big clients, and, fortunately, this was not a make-or-break deal. You have a great practice with some incredibly loyal clients, and you even have a decent residual income built up. Don't flush all of your past success down the toilet just because one large client didn't see eye to eye with you," Jen said.

She was partially right, but anyone who had been rejected by a potential new client knew the feeling of doubt it could put in your head, especially from a client like the Smiths. And it certainly didn't help that I knew they were going to do business with some other advisor they found online. I was wishing I had never even asked that question.

"Listen, Jen, I really need to figure out what I am going to do in regards to marketing, so I need some alone time to brainstorm. I know that I promised I would be home earlier, but I must get this done tonight. I will do my best to be home before the kids go to bed, OK?" I said.

She was silent for a second and then finally said, "Steve, we really need you here at home. The kids miss you, and they keep asking why you aren't here for dinner. I don't know how much longer I can do this when you are so unpredictable with our family."

"Jen, this has been one of my worst days in years, so I wouldn't even be enjoyable to be around. Please tell the kids I will see them tomorrow and I love them. I have to take care of this marketing issue. I have already put it off too long," I explained.

"Steve, I just hope you know what you are doing," she said before hanging up the phone.

Beer Brainstorm

After getting politely hung up on by my wife, I sat down at my computer and started jotting down some marketing budget numbers into a Microsoft Excel file. The only good news was that with my final payment for radio airtime in the books, I had a few thousand more dollars per month in my marketing kitty. The only problem was I had no idea how I should deploy it.

I heard of some advisors who had success buying Internet leads, but for some reason I wasn't ready for that. Especially considering the outrageous costs for a single appointment.

I already had a well-oiled seminar system, and I had certainly lost the passion to bring on another seminar platform, even if it was unique or better than what I currently had.

My other option was to think outside the box and do some old-school postcard direct mail, but I kept hearing that they just weren't pulling decent returns here in Central Florida.

After searching around the Internet for any decent lead systems, I finally decided that I needed to get some fresh air. It was already 7:15 in the evening, and I hadn't left the office yet. In fact, I even forgot to eat after the Smiths left.

I got in my car and ended up pulling up to a local pizza joint where I knew the owner. I went in and had them make me a small pepperoni and mushroom pizza. After having a beer at the bar while waiting for my pizza, I noticed a few of our friends in the back corner having dinner.

I was not in any mood to explain why I was there by myself at 8 o'clock having a beer and a pizza, so I asked the gal behind the counter if I could buy a six-pack of Budweiser and take the pizza to go.

Minutes later, I walked out the door with a warm pizza and six cold beers. This was probably the most content I felt since my shower this morning.

Once I sat down in my car, I realized that I didn't have anywhere to go eat and relax. I certainly couldn't head home with a personal pizza and a six-pack of beer, and I really didn't want to go back to the office. *Aha, I know the perfect spot.*

As I pulled up to one of the last standing orange groves, not yet ripped up to put in new homes, I felt a sense of nostalgia running through my veins.

This wasn't any ordinary orange grove; this was the spot where we snuck away as seniors in high school to drink beer and make out with our girlfriends. I had some incredible memories there, including my first beer buzz, kissing Pam Stafford, the prom queen, and even a fight I had to break up between two of my best friends, who were throwing blows left and right.

As I parked the car in between two orange trees, I got out and took in a deep whiff of the orange blossoms and fresh air. I realized how much I needed to get out and enjoy what was around me.

I was a slave to my business, and I not only neglected my wife and kids for the past few years, but I didn't even enjoying the simple things in life, like watching the stars, smelling orange blossoms, or even taking hikes, all because I was always "too busy" growing my practice.

I placed the pizza and beer down on the hood of the car, sat down on the hood, and began to eat and drink in silence while I took in everything around me.

I couldn't help but think of Jen and what she must be thinking about her crummy husband, and how long she would continue to put up with me before I'd come home one night to find she had moved out.

I thought about my kids, Ashley and Steven Jr., who barely knew their dad over the last eight years, except for weekends. There were weeks when I only saw them for an hour, and they were so preoccupied with their own teenage lives, we hardly ever got to connect and really love on each other like we did when they were younger.

It was time to make some changes at home before I woke up one day with a family that didn't even know me.

Then, I thought about my practice. *Was I really even passionate about being a financial advisor anymore?* The numbness I felt after losing the Smiths as clients made me rethink everything about my business, brand, marketing, and value to high-net-worth prospects.

I thought that perhaps I could sell my book of business, take a few months off to spend time getting to know my family again, and then get a corporate job with a salary and regular hours.

I was actually bringing in six figures a year of residual income from my AUM and life insurance business, and with a 4-5 times multiple, I could get anywhere from $500,000 to $600,000 for my practice.

Although it wouldn't be enough to fully retire—I sadly had a pitiful retirement account because I kept putting everything back into the business—it would be the start of a nice nest egg.

But then again, that would be admitting defeat at something I did well for many years. Not to mention, I really enjoyed helping people at the end of the day, I just hated the inconsistency of new clients and all the money that went into marketing.

"I just don't know what to do with my life," I said aloud.

That wasn't how I thought my future would end up... sitting by myself, as an adult, wondering where my life and my career went wrong, in the same orange grove where I once snuck beers.

I vividly remembered my first year cutting my teeth at Banker's Life and how I looked to my mentor like a young boy admires a professional baseball player.

My mentor was one of the top five money earners within the entire Banker's Life network. He had a huge five-bedroom house on a little lake, drove a well-polished BMW, had a great-looking wife and collection of fine watches – he seemed to have the best life I had ever seen firsthand.

In fact, my entire goal was to get to his level. I knew if I could have that kind of success with the big home, nice Beamer, and hot wife, my life would be complete. I mean, who would want more than that?

But there I was, many years later, and I actually had all of those things, plus some. I had a five-bedroom house with a pool, two BMWs, a watch collection, a wine collection, and a very attractive wife. Yet, somehow, I was miserable, and none of the nice "stuff" seemed to matter. My business was running me, I had no control of anything, and I hardly knew my own family.

My eyes finally adjusted to the darkness, and as I looked down at some of the old beer cans around my car that were most likely dropped by recent high school kids, I made a pact I would make some big changes, starting tomorrow.

Never again would I lose a client because of my lack of authority, either online or offline. Never again would I neglect my family, regardless of how my business was doing. And never again would

I end up in an old orange grove having to drink beers by myself while I moped about how much I hated my life and business.

"Time for change, Steve, time for change," I told myself as I pulled out of the orange grove for (hopefully) the last time in my life.

11

WHAT NOW?

By the time I arrived home at 10:30 that night, the kids were asleep, but Jen was sitting at the kitchen table having a glass of wine, clearly waiting on me to come in.

"Where you have been all night?" she said. "I actually ran into the Dixon family, who said they thought they saw you by yourself at the pizza joint. What is going on, Steve? And why do you smell like beer?"

"Lovely, I guess someone did see me in the pizza joint," I said. "Jen, today was a horrible day for me. I woke up feeling on top of the world, thinking all of my problems were going to be solved by closing one big client. But, not only did the big client back out, but it looks like they are going to do business with a competitor of mine they found online," I said. "After my catastrophic meeting, I needed time alone to think about my business, future, and, most importantly, family. I didn't particularly want to eat alone in a restaurant, so I ordered some pizza and beer and ate outside, watching the stars and thinking."

I didn't tell her I went to the old orange grove, though.

"Steve, I am sorry about the case," said Jen. "I truly am. I, more than anyone, want to see you succeed and make money. But the one thing I would rather see right now is more of you. The kids don't even bother to ask where you are for dinner; they have become accustomed to not seeing you. I sometimes wonder if you are married to your business or me. Steve, I really don't know how long we can keep doing this," she said, tears streaming down her cheeks.

"Jen, while I was thinking through all of this in the past few hours, I realized just how much I neglected you and the kids. My business has controlled me, and I have lost sight of what's really important and how much I've achieved so far. I know you've heard it before, but Jen, this time I really mean that there will be some huge changes, even if I have to sell my practice and get a normal job," I said.

She continued to cry and looked at me with bloodshot eyes, presumably from crying off and on for most of the evening. After staring at each other for a minute, Jen said, "I just don't know how many times the kids and I can keep falling for your false promises, Steve."

Back to the War Zone

After hugs and many tears on both sides, Jen and I finally went to bed. I was determined to wake up early, get in the office, map out a new game plan, and get home no later than 5:15, as promised.

My steady-as-a-rock Judy was there early as usual, and I greeted her with a big smile, along with her favorite Starbucks chai latte, which certainly must have left her wondering if I lost my mind in the last 24 hours.

"What's the occasion?" she asked.

"Today begins a new chapter at Kennedy Financial. No more complete reliance on third-party marketing and lead companies, and no more doing any kind of marketing that I am not passionate about."

Judy stared at me with a puzzled look, probably seeking more clarity.

I went on, "I'm not sure exactly which marketing strategies we will employ going forward, but I do know we have to figure it out within the next two weeks, and then I will need your full support to help me implement and maximize them."

"Steve, I am always here to help in any way I can. I'm just glad you aren't firing me! For a second, I thought this Starbucks was my going-away gift," Judy said with a smile.

"Judy, you have a job here as long as you want it. But for now, let's dig into my calendar over the next couple of weeks and block out some time each day to talk with any marketing systems and lead platforms we can find," I said.

"OK. I will meet you back in your office in a couple of minutes, and we can look over your calendar to see what future appointments we have and where we can schedule some time. I'm afraid we've neglected looking at your calendar lately, since we've only focused on the Smiths," Judy noted.

It pained me to even think about the Smiths. I couldn't believe they were actually going to do business with someone they found on the Internet. Since when did people have enough trust in a stranger to invest millions of dollars over the Internet?

I guess a lot has changed over the past few years.

Judy came into my office, and I opened up my calendar. After a few seconds of looking, I noticed an event occurring in 10 days that I had completely forgotten about.

The annual RIA convention in Las Vegas was coming up, and it was probably the last thing I needed to attend if I wanted to get my business back on track. With all the craziness at the office and at home, I forgot I booked this event months ago.

This would be my fifth trip in a row to the big RIA convention, and for me, the event seemed to be more about drinking and networking than learning anything new.

I met some really great friends from around the country, and it was nice to bounce ideas off of other RIAs and have some beers without any kids and spouses around. In many ways, it was an excuse for a bunch of us to get together and have a tamed-down version of a Vegas bachelor party.

As I reminisced about some wild RIA events, I became keenly aware that Jen would absolutely flip her lid if I went. She wasn't naïve, and she certainly knew from the brutal hangover I had last year, we did more drinking than learning in Vegas.

But at the same time, I paid $350 for the registration, $665 for the three nights at the Palazzo, and another $310 for my flight. I would hate to flush more than a thousand dollars down the toilet. Plus, I was getting really excited about a much-needed break to see some old friends, get my mind off my practice for a few days, and blow off some steam. Heck, I might even learn something this time!

Judy and I spent the next hour mapping everything out in my calendar and agreed we would interview at least one new third-party marketing company over the next week and a half; then we would narrow it down to three marketing platforms that could make sense for my practice and make a final decision.

When Judy asked if I intended to go to the RIA convention, I told her to keep it on my calendar until I was able to talk it over with Jen.

***

"You're doing what?!" Jen practically screamed. "You are going to leave me and your children here to go to some Vegas booze-fest after the talk we had last night?"

"Jen, listen, I feel like I need to be there. I always come back with new sales and marketing ideas after brainstorming with colleagues," I shot back.

Jen sat down, looking close to tears.

"Steve, we need you here. This love affair with your work is tearing us apart. Our children hardly know you; I feel like I hardly know you. Our only time together is on the weekends, and that's if we are lucky enough to be graced with your presence. Next week just really isn't the best time to leave us, Steve," she pleaded.

"Jen, I can't apologize enough for the past. All I can do is try my best to change the future. I know you must think these conferences are nothing but drinking and entertaining, but I actually come away with some great ideas," I said. "And although I admit that some of them have been less rewarding than others, I do have the sense that I am supposed to be going to this one. Not to mention, it would be like us flushing down an extra $1,100 down the toilet, since I can't recover any of the money I have already spent on the trip."

Jen was silent for a minute; then she looked up at me and said, "Steve, I hope this is worth it for you. Go have fun with your buddies in Vegas. But don't be shocked if I am not here when you get back."

12

VEGAS, BABY, VEGAS...

I was finally on the plane, and we were almost ready to take off. The last week was tough, both at home and at my office. Jen and I continued to argue quite a bit about the trip, along with numerous other things that she wanted me to do better. However, at least I kept my promise and made it home at a decent hour every night.

At the office during the week, Judy and I must have spoke with at least 20 different third-party marketing companies about everything from appointment setting, to direct mail postcards, to one-on-one dinner appointments, to Internet leads, and, finally, to buying leads from another syndicated financial radio show in my area.

All of the lead and appointment options had pros and cons, and with my 80 percent closing ratio, I knew I could succeed with most of them.

But the problem I couldn't shake was how little control I had over any of these platforms and options. It seemed the largest advisors and producers in the country had their own systems with control of their lead flows and sales funnels. None of these options gave me that. In fact, I would have been at the mercy of these companies.

It still didn't feel right, and I felt like choosing any of the companies we spoke with so far would put me back where I always was—with no power over my practice. It would be like putting a Band-Aid on something that needed surgery. I vowed I wouldn't get back in the old rut of chasing marketing companies.

The good news was that the plane ride would give me over four hours of peace and quiet, so I could brainstorm and search the web for additional marketing options. Gosh, I loved technology. Who would have thought just 10 years ago we would all be surfing the web and returning emails from 30,000 feet in the air?

After I found nothing new and drank a Bloody Mary, I took a quick siesta before landing in Vegas.

Margaritaville

It was 3 o'clock in the afternoon, Vegas time, and I just checked into my massive suite at the Palazzo. The first day of the conference was just for registration, with a 6 o'clock cocktail hour. The real event kicked off the next morning at 9 o'clock, so this was my free day.

I sent my old friend Jim Fitzpatrick a text to see if he arrived. He was a very successful RIA from Toledo, Ohio, whom I met at the same conference four years earlier. We hit it off right away, and we were friends ever since. The only times we saw each other were at this conference and occasionally on reward trips for top producers. Jim was a sharp guy and one of the best speakers I knew, and he loved to have a good time.

As I walked around the never-ending shops at the Venetian, my phone vibrated with a text from Jim. Not only was he in Vegas already, he was at Margaritavillle people watching.

"Hey, Jim!" I yelled over the sound of the street traffic.

There he was, all by himself, beer in hand, having the time of his life.

"Stevie!" Jim belted back. "Get up here and grab a cold drink, my friend."

Jim had a successful practice and was someone I always learned from. With his gift of public speaking, boisterous laugh, and magnetic personality, he grew his AUM to $305 million in 10 years. He had two full-time assistants and one junior associate who worked with his "B and C" clients.

He had what I considered my ideal practice: pretty moderate overhead, complete control of his sales pipeline, a custom mailer, and own referral system.

Not to mention that with his 60 basis points fee he charged clients, he had a nice residual income of approximately $1.8 million. No wonder he was always so happy.

"What's up, partner?" Jim said as we shook hands.

"Jim, great to see you. Looks like you found the best seat in the house," I said.

"Yes sir. Nothing like a cold beer, Jimmy Buffet music, and watching all of these freaks and tourists on the strip. I could do this for hours. Sit down and let's catch up. How has business been?" Jim asked.

I caught Jim up on everything from the radio show blowing up, to the Smiths, to my lack of control in my practice, and even to my issues at home with Jen. Jim was a good listener. He asked great questions about each topic, and I was anxious to hear his advice.

"Well, friend, sounds like you've had a wild month. Those big clients are always the toughest to land, and I hate to hear they went with a competitor… unless it was me," Jim added with his contagious laugh.

"Not funny, Jim."

"Just kidding, my man. You know I wouldn't do that to you," Jim said with full sincerity.

"So, do you have any words of wisdom before we drink too many beers?" I asked.

Jim thought for a moment. "Would it help if you spent a day with me to learn my seminar system?"

"That would be great, but I have already seen your seminar, and quite honestly, I think the seminar I have is pretty darn solid," I replied. "The one variable I could never recreate is you, Jim, and that is really what makes your seminar so successful. You could give your entire system to a dozen advisors, and not one of them would maximize it like you. I just don't think that is the solution that I am looking for. I need something that really sets me apart and gives me control of my most important piece of business: my lead and sales funnel," I said.

"Believe me," Jim said. "I understand the importance of that more than anyone. Before I decided to create my own seminar and referral system, I was just like many of the pitiful agents and advisors who were relying 100 percent on some fly-by-night lead company. The group I was using for every single one of my new prospects suddenly went belly-up and left me high and dry overnight. I took a stance the next day and decided I would never rely solely on a third-party marketing company again."

"Yep, I recall you telling me about that company when we first met," I said.

"The one piece of advice I can tell you is that once you master some sort of lead generation, magic starts happening. New doors open, floods of clients come in, and your credibility and authority skyrocket. While I hate to hear you are going through a rough time, rest assured that I would probably not be where I am today if I hadn't hit rock bottom," Jim said.

He continued, "Sadly, you usually have to learn the hard way that you really have no control over your business unless you do your own marketing. Marketing is what grows successful practices, not sales. Just look at some of the advisors and insurance agents we both know who could sell a Popsicle to an Eskimo. Yet, because they have no clue how to market, they are always at the mercy of unreliable organizations. Not to mention, they never seem to have a huge practice to sell when all is said and done. They are like the lone, hungry hunter always searching for its next prey."

"Very true," I said.

"Once I decided to take responsibility for my own marketing, never let another company run me again, and build for the long term, my business exploded, and I never looked back," Jim said. "Today, just a decade after I made all of those tough changes, my practice is bringing in over $1.5 million a year, and I know I could sell it for at least $10 million due to the residuals and the proprietary marketing systems I created."

"Jim, your advice is always worth its weight in gold. Now, I just have to discover my own secret 'marketing sauce' like you did. Hopefully, some kind of light bulb will go off over the next couple of days at this conference," I said with a mix of humor and hope.

"Well, Steve, I know that we don't have to be in a meeting until tomorrow morning, so what do you say we enjoy Vegas for old times' sake? We can skip that cocktail hour and have our own party here."

Oh boy, I thought. *It's only the first night, and I'm falling right into the same rut I always do when I come to these conferences in Vegas. As long as I remember to call Jen in the next couple of hours and drink tons of water before I go to bed, I should be good to go.*

"Jim, it's tough to say no to you, man. I'm in, but I really don't want to be out past midnight. We have a long two days ahead of us."

"Of course," Jim said with a wink. "No problem there, old Stevie."

The next thing I knew, Jim was yelling out, "Bartender, we need more tequila shots over here!"

13

CONFERENCE HANGOVERS

As my eyes slowly opened, I felt uncontrollable throbbing in my head. I looked through hazy eyes to try to find out exactly where I was this morning.

After getting my bearings, I finally remembered I was in Vegas, not in my bed at home. It had certainly been a crazy night; it was a miracle I found my room. At least I believed this was my room, based on what I could see from the bed.

I looked over at the clock and saw that it was 10:45 in the morning already.

"Crap!" I yelled out. I already missed the kick-off to the conference. With my throbbing headache and a stomach that needed some greasy food as soon as possible, I was likely to miss the entire first half of the day.

"Man, I have no business drinking like that at my age," I told myself.

My next thought was, *Did I call Jennifer last night?* I really couldn't remember.

I found my phone on the counter, along with a few $25 chips I must have forgotten to cash in. As I looked through my history of calls on the phone and saw a missed call from Jen, but there wasn't an outgoing call back to her.

Great, I thought. *She didn't even leave a message from the looks of it. She must be really ticked off at me right now. But even if I call her now, there's no way she would believe me if I tell her that I forgot to call, got up early for the meeting, and this is our first break where I can call. Man, I am really in some hot water here.*

I debated what to do; my throbbing headache prevented me from thinking at all. It hurt so much all I could think about was getting food and Advil.

I knew I had to call Jen, and that the longer that I put it off, the worse the outcome would be. I decided to tell her the truth: I ran into Jim and we got too drunk. By the time I came home the night before, it was way too late to call her.

The phone started to ring, and I felt my stomach turn from a combination of my epic hangover and a call I knew would not be fun.

After four rings, it went to her voicemail. *Thank goodness.* Now, I could just leave her a nice message that I missed her and was so sorry I didn't call her last night.

Done. I had to cure this hangover, end the throbbing headache, and get to the conference as soon as possible.

I looked at my watch and saw it was already 12:25 p.m. when I rolled up to the registration booth. I could only assume my eyes were still bloodshot, and I smelled like a mixture of day-old booze and pancakes.

I walked to the very back of the main conference room and took a seat in the last row, trying to put as much distance between me and anyone else to avoid small talk.

The current speaker was from a large institutional fund, and was discussing his theory on the bond market and why he foresaw a huge bond bubble imploding in the very near future.

As I listened to this speaker conclude, I couldn't help but reflect on how irresponsible I had been. Here I was, in Vegas, already straining the relationship with my wonderful wife with the promise I only went on this trip to get marketing ideas.

Yet, I went out and got drunk, even though I told her I wouldn't. My business would fall apart if I didn't find a marketing solution fast. And if I didn't get my act together, my marriage seemed like it might come to an end just as quickly.

The next speaker was the head of compliance for a large organization that discussed the upcoming and present compliance changes in regard to fiduciary responsibilities, outside business activities, and social media usage.

I couldn't decide what was worse—my headache or having to listen to this. After trying my best not to fall asleep, I quietly exited the back of the conference room to get some fresh air and recover before the next speaker.

While I was heading out of the conference area, I saw a familiar face approaching me.

Just great, I thought. *I bet I still reek of booze, and I can only imagine the bags under my eyes.* I could sense my body wanted much more sleep.

"Hey there, Steve. Long time no see. How the heck have you been?" asked my old friend Kevin Stern.

Kevin was one of the best wholesalers who had ever set foot in my office. He sold everything from mutual funds, to variable annuities, to REITs over the years, but his main strength was marketing. He truly "got it," and always strove to bring a new marketing idea to me whenever he came in, which was very different from the other wholesalers who just tried to wine and dine me to peddle their products.

"Hey, Kevin. I'm doing great, man," I lied. "It's been a long time since I've seen you. Are you still peddling financial products all over the South? And if so, did you get too big to come service my small office?" I asked with a smile.

"Ha! I didn't forget about you Steve. I actually accepted a pretty big promotion to run the entire East Coast distribution team for PacLife. As much as I loved face-to-face wholesaling with reps like you, I couldn't pass up this opportunity," he said.

"I understand completely," I replied. "I can honestly say you were the #1 wholesaler to ever walk into my office, so I wish you the best, and I'm sure you will knock it out of the park with your new endeavor. So, what do they have you coming to this conference for?" I asked him.

"Well, I am looking for a few new wholesalers, and these RIA conventions always seem to be a good place to find unhappy folks who are out rubbing elbows with the big sponsors.

"Also, I have been following one of the keynotes who will be speaking tomorrow in one of the breakout sessions. He talks all about authority marketing, like how to have baby boomers actually raising their hands to work with you (instead of the other way around), and how to take advantage of the Internet to spread your message and create prospects.

"His name is Dave Utley, and you should definitely make it to that session. I read his last two books, and they are pretty powerful marketing tools," Kevin said passionately.

"Interesting," I said. "Never heard of the guy, but that doesn't mean much. I am no marketing guru."

Thankfully, Kevin had no idea how bad of a marketer I was. I also thought to myself that if Kevin, one of the best marketers and salesmen in the industry, thought this highly of a speaker, then I really needed to hear this guy.

"I think you will like him and his candid approach to how to market like an authority in the 21st century. Not to mention, he is a hoot when he's onstage," Kevin said.

"That's great, man. I really appreciate the heads up, and it was great running into you here. I assume you will be in the breakout with this Dave Utley, so I will try to sit next to you so we can catch up more," I said.

"You are certainly welcome to sit next to me, but this session will be unlike any other you have been to. The only person talking will be Dave, and I can almost assure you that the last thing you will want to do is chitchat with me while he is speaking," Kevin explained.

"Should be a nice break compared to some of the boring sessions in the past. Looking forward to it," I said.

"No doubt. And don't forget to bring a good pen and a pad of paper. You are going to want to take down everything this guy says," Kevin said. He shook my hand, and we parted ways.

After talking with Kevin, I pulled out my phone to see if I missed a call from Jen. Nothing. *That's not good.*

I decided to head back to my room and give her a call before I took a 20-minute power nap, hoping it would get me back in my normal groove. It rang through to her voicemail, and I left her another loving, apologetic message for missing her call the night before.

Now it was time for a power nap.

That nap was almost magical; I woke up feeling like a new man. Perhaps it had something to do with my excitement about this marketing guy Dave Utley who I was going to see the next day. I was hoping this could be the solution to my marketing problems. It could even be the reason I felt I should go to the conference in the first place, which certainly wasn't to get as drunk as I had the night before.

It was 30 minutes since I tried last, so I reached for my phone to see if Jen had returned my call

I had one new text, but it was from Jim asking if I wanted to go out with him and a couple of fund managers, whose jobs were to entertain reps like us.

Not a chance.

The pain of going out on the town with Jim was all too recent, and I wasn't about to jeopardize the meeting the next morning. I replied back that I was going to lay low, as he had put a hurting on me last night.

Since Jen didn't attempt to call me back, I figured I might as well go hit the conference again and hope to learn something.

14

MEET DAVE UTLEY, MARKETING GURU

I showed up five minutes early to the breakout meeting with Dave. If the guy was so well regarded as a marketing expert, I could only imagine I would not be the only person who wanted to see him.

Surprisingly, it wasn't as packed as I thought it would be. In fact, it wasn't packed at all. I became a little less excited and wondered if Kevin gave this guy too much credit. Perhaps Kevin was related to him—or just trying to help someone new to the speaking circuit get more attendance. Either way, I was there.

While I waited for the doors to open, I reflected on the rest of the previous afternoon. I went back to the auditorium after my nap and returned to my seat in the back.

The last two speakers were interesting; however, I didn't learn anything about marketing, which was really all I could focus on.

If I didn't learn anything in Dave Utley's presentation, then the entire conference would be a waste of time. The next day would be the last, and the only things that usually happened were an award ceremony, a panel, and a final cocktail party.

"Well, here goes nothing," I said to myself, as the doors to the breakout room opened. They ushered the small group of us waiting outside through. I saw my friend Kevin in the back of the line and gave him a nod. He cut in line and stood next to me. "You are going to love this dude," he said. "He really *is* a marketing genius."

"I sure hope so, Kevin. But why are so few advisors here if this guy is as exceptional as you say?" I inquired.

"Great question," he said. "Dave Utley is one of the top marketing consultants for many of the fastest-growing Inc. 100 companies in the country. That has been his niche; he tries to avoid working with large public and bureaucratic businesses and focuses on fast-growing independent groups that have cash, momentum, and want to take things to an entirely new level of growth."

He continued, "This is actually the first time he has ever done anything in the RIA space, or really even in the financial services industry, that you and I are accustomed to."

"So, my guess is that since most RIAs and financial advisors have their heads in the sand when it comes to studying and reading about marketing outside of our industry, they have probably never heard of Dave," explained Kevin.

"Even though I am certain the conference paid dearly to have him here, I am betting there was some political tension to keep their old-school speakers as the keynotes, so Dave was stuck with this small breakout room," Kevin said. "But trust me, this is a huge deal that we get him all to ourselves. It's like going to a private Jimmy Buffet concert with only 75 other people."

"I don't even want to think about Margaritaville after my first evening here in Vegas. Regardless, I hope you are right," I said.

The Marketing Presentation That Changed Everything

As the group of 75 to 85 of us sat down around the room built for 150 in the Palazzo conference area, you could hear small talk going on among different advisors while we waited for Dave Utley.

I was sitting next to Kevin and another advisor he used to work with.

We were talking about the future of variable annuities after so many of the carriers pulled out of the space, when all of a sudden a booming voice came through the loud speakers, as if a thunderbolt came through the room. A few people even jumped out of their chairs slightly – no one saw it coming.

We all turned around to the back of the auditorium to see a charismatic-looking man dressed in trendy blue jeans, New Balance sneakers, and a long-sleeved shirt with the sleeves rolled up. He had longer hair than any other speaker at the conference, and he seemed the opposite of the Wall Street type we usually saw on stage.

"Certainly not what I expected Dave Utley to look like," I whispered to Kevin.

Dave started his walk toward the stage. As he looked around at the half-filled room, he said loudly, "I guess the other advisors are either too drunk, too broke, or too dumb to realize they should be in here this morning."

The entire room exploded in laughter; we were magnetized instantly by this out-of-place but captivating speaker.

He continued as he walked up to the stage area. "Advisors, I can promise you today, this presentation will not only be completely different than any other, but you *will* learn something about marketing.

"Unless, that is, you fall asleep. And if I even sense anyone dozing off in this presentation, I can assure you it will be the last time."

We all chuckled.

Dave continued by saying, "The presentation you are about to see is a bit unique because it is only five slides. And yes, I realize we have a full hour here today. But these are no ordinary slides.

"In fact, what you are going to see are virtually the same five slides that one of my multibillion-dollar clients, who pays me a handsome retainer each year, got to see last week. And her executives were blown away.

"My goal is that you leave fully understanding that you don't need more sales tools and tips, or more letters behind your name to grow your business.

"And another shocker for some of you who complain about a lack of prospects is that there is *not* any shortage of prospects. In fact, it is just the opposite. Today, there are more prospects looking for solid financial advice from a trustworthy advisor than ever.

"The problem is they don't like how they are communicated with. Most of you have no idea how to speak to prospects and attract them to your practice. At the end of the day, what you all *really* need is marketing help.

"My friend Dan Kennedy says, if you believe you are a financial advisor, then you are greatly mistaken. You are actually in the business of marketing financial services, and unless you fully understand that, you will forever struggle to hit lofty goals in this industry.

"And what I have found with professionals like financial planners and advisors is that you struggle with the following four things I want to try and solve for you today:

> *"You don't have enough qualified prospects to see each week, month, or year.*
>
> *"You really stink at prospecting and marketing.*
>
> *"Your sales activity and total production is lower than you want it to be, especially when you consider how much you spend on your practice.*
>
> *"Your bank account is not as impressive as you hoped it would be at this point in your career.*

"Today, not only will you walk away with some proven marketing ideas to help you solve these problems, but I am going to show you how to do it. I am going to give you the keys to your ideal clients' hearts," he said with a wink and chuckle.

"The big question is, will you have what it takes to implement and take action, or will you be like the majority of advisors who get excited about the new information they hear at a conference, but then go home and get back in the swing of their old routines, the very routines you know need a-fixin'?" Dave said.

"Now you know why I feel sorry for the bozo advisors who decided to sleep in or play on their smartphones while pretending to listen to someone talk about compliance or how boring the industry is," he said.

The room was engulfed with laughter again.

He kept going, "Well, since we only have an hour and five whole slides to go through, let's get started."

More soft laughter filled the room.

As he cranked up the projector on the big screen, we saw two huge words in all caps: **AUTHORITY MARKETING**.

"Let's talk about authority for a minute," Dave said. "Can I see a show of hands for who believes they have authority?"

Ninety percent of the room, including myself, slowly raised our hands high.

"OK," Dave said. "That's what I figured. Let's hear from some of you on why you believe you are an authority. Anyone want to volunteer before I start picking people?"

One of the advisors up in the front raised his hand and said, "I consider myself an authority because I'm a recognized name on the largest radio station in Dallas, Texas."

"OK. Who else?" asked Dave.

Another advisor spoke up. "I'm an authority because I coauthored a book."

"Who else?"

"I am an authority because I'm President of the Chamber of Commerce in my town," came another voice.

"Keep going," Dave said.

"I am an authority because I am a CFA and CFP," one more advisor chimed in.

"Good stuff, everyone," said Dave. "Now, let me tell you why authority is so crucial before I share how you can achieve the utmost authority going forward in today's environment."

He clicked ahead to the next slide, and up popped huge pictures of Suze Orman, Jim Kramer, and Dave Ramsey.

You could hear some "boos" and other negative chatter around the room.

"So, based on the whispering and booing I hear from the crowd, I assume you all know who these three people are," said Dave. "Who thinks these three financial celebrities have more authority than you?"

Every single hand in the audience went up, including mine.

Dave continued, "And why is this the case? Why do these three averaging-looking, yet highly identifiable people have more authority than you?"

"Because of the media," said one advisor.

"Because they have their own TV shows," said another.

"OK," said Dave. "Those are all good thoughts. Let's look at this another way before I reveal to you how they were able to get so much authority."

Dave pointed and began to speak to someone in the audience, "You, sir, with the yellow tie. I recall you didn't raise your hand when asked if you believe you have authority. I don't need to know why, but I want to confirm that you believe these three celebrities have more authority than you."

The timid advisor in the yellow tie nodded.

"Well, how much more authority do they have? I want you to tell us, in a percentage, how much more authority Dave Ramsey has than you," Dave instructed.

"Ah, I don't know. Perhaps 500 percent more authority than me?" offered the yellow tie guy.

There were some chuckles in the audience.

"Hmmm... 500 percent more authority," Dave said as he rubbed his chin. "That is a lot of authority compared to you, Mr. Yellow Tie.

"OK. Next question. Mr. Yellow Tie, do you consider yourself 500 times dumber or 500 times less educated or informed than Ramsey?" Dave asked and paused for effect.

Mr. Yellow Tie immediately interjected and said, "Heck no. Ramsey isn't that smart. In fact, I think I'm just as smart and certainly more informed on financial products than he will ever be."

"Very interesting," Dave said thoughtfully. "Well then, let me ask the entire audience a question. Is there anyone here who considers himself or herself smarter and better able to give financial advice than Dave Ramsey?"

The entire audience raised their hands, including me. I respected Dave Ramsey a lot; I read his books, and some friends even got out of debt because of him. However, he was no financial planner. I truly believed I knew more than him when it came to estate planning and creating overall retirement plans.

"Wow!" Dave exclaimed. "One hundred percent of you believe you are smarter and better suited to give financial advice than Dave Ramsey. Yet, not a single person believes they have as much authority.

"I am willing to bet that if we walked out on the street here in Vegas and made 100 random pedestrians choose between you and Dave Ramsey to help them plan for retirement, they all would pick Ramsey. Anyone disagree?"

The room fell silent.

"Well then... perhaps I was wrong. It looks like the dumb ones actually showed up for my meeting," Dave said with a grin.

Everyone laughed and waited for what Dave was going to say next.

Dave continued, "Actually, you are all probably correct with your assessment, and that is what I anticipated you would say. So, let's take a look at why this crazy phenomenon happened, and how these three financial gurus were able to get authority over people like you, who are clearly more qualified."

"Let me first say I've had the pleasure of meeting all three of these financial celebrities over the past few years, and you are correct – not a single one of them is smarter, better looking, or more knowledgeable than most of you.

"I say 'most of you,' because I noticed a couple of men with some pretty alarming mustaches that make it tough for me to say you are better looking than even Jim Kramer."

Everyone laughed and looked around at the handful of men with mustaches in the crowd.

Dave kept going, "In reality, these three people aren't superheroes. But they do have *mucho* authority in the eyes of consumers. And it really boils down to the fact that these people had the foresight to be givers of information and education when none of us even considered doing that for free. They were pioneers of the marketing mantra: help others, rather than sell hard with misleading advertising.

"Whether you want to believe it or not, these three people have more trust with the average consumer than most of you will have in your entire careers, because they gave out information openly, shared their stories, impacted millions, and created so much goodwill with their followers that many of them will buy and do anything asked.

"Now THAT is some serious authority," Dave said. "But what you don't see is that it didn't come easy or overnight, like many of us assume. It was from years of doing what I call content marketing, or authority marketing. Basically, sharing their insight and stories, and helping as many people as they could, regardless of if they sold anything. And before you knew it, doors started opening.

"I can already tell from this audience you don't want to hear me talk about Orman, Ramsey, and Kramer for the entire hour. That's why I purposely put them here in the first slide to fire you up and get your minds going. Now, it's time to get into the good marketing stuff, the stuff you came for and can change your practice.

"Before I begin, I have one quick story to tell you about authority, just so you can get a grasp on how powerful it is for getting your prospects and clients to take action," Dave said. "I want to point out that just like any powerful force, it can be used for good—and for evil. I do not condone or promote ever using it for manipulative or illegal purposes. And please, do not think for a moment after you hear this true story you should mislead people. If you do, I hope you end up in jail. On that note, here goes slide two."

I looked up on the screen and saw a picture of a security officer in front of an ATM on the side of a bank, holding a sign that read, "Out Of Order—Give Deposits to Guard On Duty."

Dave looked out at the audience and said, "This is a true story about testing the limits of authority. A television reporter decided to see what would happen if he dressed up like a fake security guard, with a nicely polished gold badge and uniform, and held the sign you see on the screen.

"So, get this: Patrons started showing up, and every time the fake officer pointed to the sign, smiled, and asked them if they wanted to make a deposit or withdrawal. And customer after customer complied; they gave this fake guard/reporter their account, Social Security, PIN, and debit card numbers... everything."

Dave continued while we all sat in bewilderment, "And 9 out of 10 people complied with no hesitation. Only one hesitated and asked a few extra questions, but even he complied after a few minutes.

"Isn't that crazy!" Dave yelled. "Have you ever heard of a bank that operates this way? Of course not! But after the reporter revealed the prank and deception to the unsuspecting bank visitors, and asked them why in the world they gave all of their information, each replied with a similar answer: "Because of the uniform. Because of the sign."

"In other words, the security guard with a badge had so much *perceived* authority that 9 out of 10 consumers didn't suspect anything. Now, THAT is authoritative power, my friends."

15

PERMISSION-BASED MARKETING

Slide #3 popped up on the screen; it was a picture of a middle-aged woman holding a box of Tide in her hands in front of what looked to be the entrance of her laundry room.

We stared in silence for a few seconds before Dave began. "Let me see a show of hands: How many of you love commercials? Meaning, you love being interrupted during your favorite shows, sporting events, and so on."

Not a single hand went up.

"Interesting," Dave said with a hint of sarcasm. "Did you know the average American is exposed to over 3,000 unique and interrupting marketing messages every single day? Yet, not one person in this room likes to be marketed to this way. Well, show me, with some hands, how many of you hate commercials so much that you have TiVo or another form of DVR you use to skip through commercials."

We all raised our hands. "I can't stand commercials," I said in a hushed tone.

"Hmmm," Dave pondered. "That is remarkable! Almost every single person hates commercials so much that not only do they not watch them, but they actually *pay money* every month for a service to skip them.

"Well, what about the radio? Do you like to jam to your favorite song on the radio, only to have the good times abruptly ended by a radio ad?" Dave asked. "Let me see some hands."

No hands went up.

"Better yet, do any of you pay for services like Sirius XM to avoid commercials and get the music you want, when you want it, without being rudely interrupted?"

My hand shot up, as did about half the hands in the room.

"OK, moving on," Dave said. "How many of you love getting spam mail? This could be junk mail at home or spam emails in your inbox. Basically anything that shows up that you didn't request. Come on, raise 'em nice and high."

Not a single hand went up.

"Very interesting," Dave said with his token sarcasm. "Let's talk about something a little more 'new age.' Who loves clicking on a YouTube video and being forced to wait 5 to 30 seconds for the ad to play before you can watch the video?"

Everyone remained silent.

"Wow. This is very interesting stuff," Dave said. "One more quick question on these YouTube commercials. Has anyone in this room ever found the forced ads so irresistible that you clicked on them and forgot about the video?"

We shook our heads.

"Well, I just have to keep trying until I can get some hands in the air. Do any of you enjoy landing on a website and immediately seeing several pop-up ads on the screen? Don't be shy."

Not a single hand went up again, and you could hear a few chuckles around the room.

"So, you mean to tell me that not a single one of you enjoys or appreciates TV commercials, radio advertisements, junk mail, spam email, forced video advertisements, or pop-up ads? And in some cases you hate it so much you are willing to pay money for it to go away?"

I nodded, as did many of the other attendees in the room.

"Well, darn it. Let me try one more thing," Dave said with a slight laugh. "Here is what I need you to do. I need you to raise your right hand as high as you can if you hear me say a certain type of marketing that *you* have personally paid for to market your practice in the last 12 months. Meaning, if I list off a type of marketing that you have personally paid for in order to create a lead for yourself, raise your right hand. If you hear me say a second type of marketing you paid for in the last 12 months, then raise your left hand as well. Got it?"

"Yes," we all agreed.

"Let's discuss TV commercials really quickly. How many of you have paid for TV commercials in the past 12 months?" Dave asked.

Three advisors raised their right hands.

"Now, let me see some hands if you have personally spent money on radio advertisements in the last 12 months," Dave asked.

A big chunk of hands went up.

"OK, let's see some hands if you have ever spent any money on direct mail, also known as junk mail, that went to someone's house who did not specifically ask you to send them something."

All of the advisors in the room now had at least their right hands up, and a couple of them already had two hands up. You could start to hear some slightly uncomfortable laughter as we saw where Dave was going.

"Holy crap, that is everyone in the room already," Dave exclaimed. "Well, let's keep going to see just how bad this gets."

"Raise your left hand if you have ever done any of the following advertising. Have you ever bought an email list and blasted emails to people who didn't ask for them, paid for advertisements on YouTube videos, or had pop-ups appear on your website or another site?"

As I looked around the room, about 80 percent had both hands in the air, including me. Dave remained quiet; I could tell he wanted us to look around and grasp what was happening.

He finally spoke. "Does anyone see an issue here?"

The room nodded in unison.

"I couldn't get a single one of you to tell me you liked or even remotely enjoyed others marketing to you with outdated and interrupting tactics, yet, you are all guilty of doing it to your prospects. And about 80 percent of you are guilty on multiple counts," he said.

"And you wonder why your marketing continues to suffer, why you have to keep spending more money each year to get the same results, and why these old methods aren't working like they used to. It's because no one likes to be sold this way anymore.

"This is not to say these methods don't work, because many of them do. However, they don't work like they used to.

"This isn't your fault, though. Because back in the days when we didn't have so many choices, when there were only 12 TV channels, four magazine subscriptions to choose from, one news station, and fewer advertisements in our faces, these old methods worked... and they worked extremely well! But as we continued to get more choices, thus more advertisements, we became numb to them—and in many cases resented or shut them out.

"The sad part is, these old tactics are still taught in our schools by teachers that only know one way to advertise. There are many third-party marketing and advertising agencies owned and operated by people who grew up with, and only know, this one way to market. And I am here to tell you that this method is not only dying, it is dying quickly.

"We call this *interruption marketing*. For decades, it has worked at interrupting people to try to get them to look at your product or service. And ironically, when interruption advertising first came out, it was considered cool and exciting, because no one had seen anything like it before. Some of you might be old enough to remember when commercials first came out on TV.

"For you younger advisors, this was back when there were four channels total to choose from. In essence, interruption marketing was a great way to introduce people to new products and services they weren't aware of. Keep in mind, this was well before we had the Internet.

"But over the years, three things have changed and altered the way we respond to marketing.

"Number one is that today's adults have a much better grasp on the value of time. Never before in history have we had so much to do and so many different ways to do things, but so little time. And because of this busy and ever-moving society we have become, people now cherish and respect their own personal time like never before. And when you interrupt their time or take it away, you risk ticking off a potential customer. Furthermore, because of this appreciation for time, consumers are willing to pay for more time to enjoy what they want to be doing.

"The second thing that has changed is choices. Back 100 years ago, you had one choice of car with one color option: black. Similarly, you had just a small handful of choices in soda pop, and no one even thought of things like bottled water. Today, there are thousands of soft drinks and hundreds of different choices in bottled water. Back then, people either read *Time Magazine, Newsweek, TV Guide,* or *National Geographic.* Today, there are tens of thousands of magazines that cater to the smallest niches imaginable. And let's not forget about the 900–plus TV channels we all need to keep us happy.

"All of these choices have brought more advertisements with every outlet. So instead of having just a handful of soft drink commercials and beer commercials like we did 60 years ago, we now have thousands of different soft drinks and adult beverages vying for our attention with interruption marketing. The same goes for every kind of product or service you can imagine.

"You see, the amount of advertisements and 'buy now' pitches have massively expanded and continue to grow at a crazy rate. We even have TVs showing us commercials while we pump gas.

"But the big problem with this is, our ability to absorb and comprehend information has not expanded. Our minds are working harder and harder trying to filter, tune out, and even outright avoid much of it. No wonder we all hate commercials and advertisements so much today!" Dave exclaimed.

"The third thing that changed is our ability to research, find out the truth, and locate anything we can possibly imagine using the Internet. If I bust a hole in my shoe, do you think I head straight over to the TV and wait for a shoe commercial to tell me which new ones to buy? Heck no! I go directly to the Internet and start doing some research, including getting instant price comparisons and other customer reviews.

"Many of you are probably asking yourself, what is the answer to fix this issue?" Dave went on. "Well, the answer lies in something called *permission-based marketing*, also known as *trust-based marketing*. It revolves around three main principles my friend Seth Godin describes in his book, *Permission Marketing*:

- Anticipated—as in, people look forward to hearing from you.
- Personal—the marketing message is directly related to the individual, not just throwing as much marketing jargon as possible up against a wall and seeing what sticks.
- Relevant—the marketing must be something the prospect is actually interested in.

"Let me give an example using something each of us has been a part of at one point or another in our lives—dating.

"In the dating world, interruption marketing is like the cheese-ball guy who goes up to random women at the bar, who are clearly having a conversation and enjoying their current company, then interrupts them, puts on a big smile, brags about himself for a few minutes, and gives out his card with his personal cell phone number on the back, like he is doing them a favor.

"For all of you ladies in the room, does this kind of marketing work?" Dave asked.

"Not a chance!" yelled one woman in the back.

"Exactly right," said Dave, laughing. "In order to get the first date or even a call back, you must give women something of value or a genuine reason to see you again. And it probably doesn't help to rudely interrupt them during their conversations.

"As I mentioned earlier, we all cherish our time, and no sane woman is going to waste one of her evenings unless she is somewhat certain you are interesting enough to join on a date.

"And if your goal is long term, to get married (or in your case, win a client for life), starting the relationship off with interruption marketing is like shoving your tongue down a girl's throat as soon as you meet her at the bar. Chances are, it won't work out.

"Now that we all agree interruption marketing doesn't work like it used to, let's talk about how you can start implementing permission marketing into your practice.

"Let me start off by saying that everything we will discuss from this point forward will be about different ways to market, ask permission, and grow your practice using the Internet.

"Whether you want to believe it or not, society pressures and expectations have created an environment where you and your business don't exist if you can't be found on the Internet. Plain and simple."

Your Website

"All right, time for more trivia. Please raise your hand if you currently have some sort of website, even if it looks horrible," Dave asked.

Every single advisor had their hands raised. Despite the Smiths' research, I *did* have a website – it was just an embarrassing one that needed work. I purchased a template website about two years prior and had them slap up my logo, picture, and a brief "about me" section. It hadn't changed one bit since then.

"OK, now keep your hand raised if you are currently generating and nurturing prospects from your website," Dave said.

All of the hands went down except for one advisor's.

"Congrats to you, sir," Dave said as he looked at the one person with his hand up. "The bad news for you is that I am about to teach all of these competitors how to do the same."

The entire room roared with laughter.

"Let's begin," Dave said. "The great news I have is you really don't need a flashy, expensive website with elaborate pictures and graphics. In fact, those kinds of sites rarely convert and nurture leads and prospects.

"But what you do need, and what you should set out to accomplish, is to have a website that is chock full of permission marketing. This means your website must be personal, relevant, specific, and constantly adding value. It should be focused on getting complete strangers to give you their information in return for something of worth to them, which begins the whole permission- and trust-based marketing sequence.

"How do you accomplish this with a website, you ask?

"First, identify your absolute ideal client and then speak directly to that person in every single message, blog, and idea that you post on your site. You must understand first and foremost that if you are trying to be something to everyone on your site, you will quickly be nothing to anyone.

"When people are online, they are looking for something specific. And when it comes to financial advice, they are usually looking for something specific that is going to have an immediate benefit to them.

"This might sound shocking, but consumers aren't out surfing the web aimlessly, praying that some marketing message will pop up out of the blue and influence them to buy something they probably don't need.

"This is just not the way buyers want to be sold. Instead, they prefer to make up their minds based on their own information gathering.

"Yet, I see too many financial advisors who make the mistake of creating their sites all about themselves. They talk about their accomplishments, integrity, time in the business, and awesome products. Let it be known that consumers could not care less about that stuff. They would rather work with a robot that gives them countless benefits and makes the site all about the consumer than with stuffy veteran advisors who have every designation known to man, but only talk about themselves.

"Ladies, it would be like going on a date with the same guy who tried to shove his tongue down your throat, while also only talking about himself and never asking you a single question about your life and interests.

"When will we learn that people are only in it for themselves when they are online? They do not care about you!" Dave exclaimed.

I started thinking to myself that this permission marketing made complete sense. However, I had no idea how to build websites—or how to implement any of Dave's suggestions, for that matter.

He continued, "The next piece you must address on your site is precisely how you help your ideal client. An easy formula I teach my clients is:

"I help ________ do/create/build ________, so that they may ______________.

"Let me put it in action for you, so you can see how simple, yet effective, this is.

"Personally, I would have a video of myself at the top of the home page, so visitors could not only get a nice welcome, but also see me and start to immediately build a relationship.

"Here is what my video would say: **Thanks for visiting Utley Financial. My entire mission is to help** baby boomers **create** a contractually guaranteed lifetime income stream in retirement, **so that they may** live out their retirement dreams, such as traveling, spending time with family, and living worry free.

"See how easy that was? And when someone comes to my site, they know precisely who I can help, what I do, and what I help people achieve.

"If that person isn't a baby boomer, then he or she will probably leave. And that is perfectly fine with me. Remember, I can't help everyone.

"This is one of the hardest pieces to digest about your site, and many of my business clients cringe when I force them to do this; yet it's proven to work 100 percent of the time. A website isn't perfect unless it detracts the non-ideal prospects just as quickly as it attracts the ideal prospects. And the only way to do that is to let people know right off the bat whom your site can help.

"The next piece is to have a powerful call-to-action on the home page. And by the way, 'book an appointment with me' or 'call now for a free consultation' is a garbage call-to-action. You might as well write that you are a used car salesman and want to date their only daughter."

The entire room chuckled.

"The call-to-action needs to be something that you give your visitors in return for their information. And it better be incredibly rich with benefits. It could be a free report, an e-book, a video series, a Kindle book, your recording seminar presentation, or anything else that is of value. Keep in mind that the most important piece is going to be the headline describing the benefits, not the features, of what they will receive in return for giving their names and email addresses.

"This will tie into an auto-responder, such as Aweber, Infusionsoft, or MailChimp, which will automatically capture their information and store it for you, along with emailing them the free report, video, or what-have-you. The auto-responder can even continue to drip email on your leads for eternity. We will talk about this a little bit more on the next slide.

"Now some of you might be wondering how to get people to your site once you have all of this built. There are really two ways.

"One is to do what is called *native advertising* on places like Facebook, LinkedIn, and Google. Native advertising is you giving value and benefit to your prospects in return for their permission to keep contacting them. They are called native ads because they blend into the surroundings of the platform and don't stick out like a sore thumb. These native ads look like real content, the stuff we all seek out on the Internet that informs, inspires, and even entertains.

"The opposite of a native advertisement would be an ad like the one for Tide, just screaming that is has 10 percent more whitening power than the competition. Who cares, and who is the judge of that? People are bombarded with ads today, and unless it has clear, precise value and benefit, their brains are accustomed to tuning it out.

"The second option to get traffic is through content marketing, also known as organic search engine marketing (SEM). This is where you create valuable content in a blog, video, or some combination of the two.

"My friends Joe Pulizzi and Newt Barrett describe an incredibly powerful content marketing formula in their book, '*Get Content, Get Customers,*' known as the B.E.S.T formula. It looks like this:

- *Behavioral.* Everything you communicate with your customers has a purpose. What do you want them to do?
- *Essential.* Deliver information your best prospects need if they are to succeed at work or in life.
- *Strategic.* Your content marketing efforts must be an integral part of your overall business strategy.
- *Targeted.* You must target your content precisely, so that it is truly relevant to your buyers.

"I teach a great course on how to maximize your content to be found, also known as search engine optimization (SEO), and it really isn't as hard or as mysterious as many people make it out to be.

"But the key with all of this content marketing is to always add value, state a problem that your ideal prospect is having, agitate it a little bit to spell out what will happen if she doesn't fix the problem, and then tell her to imagine what it will be like when her problem is solved... with your help, of course.

"This is known as *problem, agitate, solve,* and it is incredibly powerful stuff. Here is a quick example that might hit home for you. Let me go up on the whiteboard and draw it out.

Dave made his way over to the whiteboard, while I sat ready to take down some more notes. I looked down to see that I was already through over 15 pages of notes so far. And for the first time in my career, I was actually getting excited about marketing. I couldn't believe I had been looking at it so wrong, like it was some mundane advertising scheme this entire time. Perhaps this permission-based content and authority marketing were the things I was looking for.

Dave began speaking again at the whiteboard. "OK, I will state the problem first, and it usually needs to be in the form of an eye-catching, powerful headline. How about this?" He quickly wrote a short paragraph.

Problem:
Are you sick and tired of chasing leads, watching your marketing budget increase just to keep up with last year's results, and wondering when you will ever get control of your marketing and sales pipeline?

"Can anybody here relate to this problem?" Dave asked.

I looked around to see tons of heads nodding, and I was relieved other advisors felt the same misery I was facing. *How could we all be such bad marketers?* I wondered.

"Now, I am going to agitate it with some bullet points I would use in the copy of a blog, video, or something similar," said Dave as he continued writing.

Agitate:
You have no control of your sales pipeline
You will continue to spend more and more every year, as the old ways of marketing as a financial advisor are slowly dying
The fastest-growing financial advisors who truly understand marketing are doing it online using permission-based marketing
Your ideal clients are online, and you aren't
At some point, you will be extinct if you aren't found online

"I think you see my point. You want to agitate it enough so that you get your prospect thinking really hard about how this problem is starting to spin out of control and how it must be fixed," Dave explained to us.

"Finally, you throw her the life raft, which needs to be your solution. Now, what I have found is the word 'imagine' is one of the most powerful words to get someone thinking and envisioning how much better her life would be.

"Here is what I mean, using our example." He then wrote some more on the whiteboard.

Solve:
By using permission-based content marketing in your practice, you can finally get complete control of your leads and your sales pipeline. Just imagine what it will feel like when you can spend less on marketing,

never have to rely on third-party marketing companies, and end up writing more business and helping more people than you thought possible.

"Powerful stuff, huh?" said Dave.

I was nodding, and so was everyone else. Powerful, indeed. I couldn't wait to get home and try some of this out, and we still had two slides to go!

Dave started back up again, "Finally, remember that in all of your marketing endeavors, you must add value and have a strong call-to-action.

"I will leave you with this great analogy of permission marketing from Seth Godin in his book, *Permission Marketing*, before we move on to the next slide," Dave said.

"Think of an interruption marketer as a hunter and a permission marketer as a farmer.

"Hunting down prospects involves loading a gun with bullets and shooting until you hit something. It can certainly work, and it has proven to work for many years. However, some days, or even weeks, you might go without ever seeing anything to kill. So, hunting is a never-ending cycle of always trying to eat what you kill, and it certainly isn't scalable.

"On the other hand, farming for prospects involves a lot of work, such as hoeing, planting, watering, and then harvesting. It is infinitely more predictable than hunting; however, it does take regular focus and attention. But once you understand how to farm, it is more scalable than any other way to get food. And once you get good at it, you can plant more seeds and harvest more crops, just like clockwork, each year."

16

"LET TRUTH AND TRANSPARENCY CHANGE EVERYTHING"

We looked up intently at the screen as Dave changed the slide. What came up was a picture of a guy with a crew cut standing in front of a big fiberglass pool.

Dave started talking, "Now, you might be wondering why I have a normal-looking dude standing next to a big pool up here. Let me explain.

"I have consulted and worked with over 400 different companies in over 185 different industries to improve their marketing. Can any of you guess what almost every single company said before I proved them wrong by implementing my marketing ideas?"

No one said anything.

"No guesses, huh?" Dave said. "Well, let me just tell you then. Before showing all of these different companies this idea of permission-based, content-driven, authority marketing, almost all of the companies I consult initially tell me, 'Dave, that is great and all, *but our business is different.*'

"Yet, time and time again, I prove them wrong. From the tax return company, to the chain of karate dojos, to the guitar store, to the utility company, to the business that sells fishing lures, to the pet grooming chain, to the financial advisory practice... there is simply no business that is different and can't explode when utilizing this kind of marketing I am discussing today."

Hmm, I thought. *I guess he is probably right. We all keep thinking we are so different as financial advisors, but it all comes down to the same marketing principles that guide and grow any company. This guy is good.*

Dave cranked back up, "So, this gentleman on the slide's name is Marcus Sheridan. I read about him in the foreword of a book that I highly encourage all of you to buy in the next 24 hours, called *Youtility* by Jay Baer.

"Let me tell you about this guy Marcus really quickly and what he went through as an entrepreneur, just like many of you.

"Marcus was part owner of a company based in Virginia that sold nothing but in-ground fiberglass swimming pools. They were doing just fine as a small business until the financial collapse of 2008. Because, guess what, when people lose 30 to 40 percent of their assets, the last thing on their minds is buying a new swimming pool.

"Basically overnight, the pool business dried up. Just weeks later, their employees were sent home with nothing to do and became overdrawn on their accounts in a very short amount of time, with literally no new business coming in."

Wow. And I thought I had it bad with my practice.

Dave continued, "So, Marcus had a big decision to make. He could either admit failure, shut down the office, sell their inventory, and start over, or he could go out on a limb and try the kind of permission marketing I have been telling you about.

"Believe me, if you don't think a pool company that only built pools in a small radius between Virginia and Maryland thought, *but we are different, and how could blogging and content marketing work for us?* then you would be mistaken.

"At this point, what did they have to lose?

"So Marcus, who had never blogged a day in his life, started his first-ever blog for River Pools and Spas. And since he didn't know what to write about, he decided to just start replying to his customers' and prospects' questions and posting the answers on the blog. He had already answered most of these questions over the phone, email, and even face to face, so he figured that if one person had a certain question about swimming pools, there must certainly be others out there with the same question.

"And boy, was he right. After well over 100 blog posts of simply doing nothing but stating a question as the title and then answering it as honestly as possible without selling or bragging about his company's pools, the site started getting some organic traffic from the search engines. Marcus' plan began to work.

"He was still working 60 hours per week, trying to do anything he could to drum up business for his company, so he had to write these posts late at night while his family was asleep. His goal was to put new content on the blog that answered people's questions every single week.

"Here is the transformation he saw with his company all because of a blog, according to Marcus himself. I will pull them up on a slide for you so you can take notes."

The slide changed and we saw the following bullet points:

Pre-blogging sales cycle for River Pools:

1. Potential customers received numerous interruption marketing direct mail pieces from River Pools.
2. In some cases, they had a telemarketer making outbound calls to people who had expressed interest in buying a pool in the past.
3. At one point or another, due to some form of interruption marketing, the company got the pool prospect on the phone and they agreed for an at-home appointment, where the pool expert would come and "sell them."
4. The pool expert, usually one of the owners, such as Marcus, would show up at the house for the sales appointment.
5. Because the prospect was usually caught off guard by having a sales appointment, Marcus found that their knowledge about pools (different types, costs, maintenance, accessories) was so poor he would have to spend multiple hours with them just addressing their basic concerns at the kitchen table. This was all before he could get to the point where he could start talking about what it was they really wanted and how he could give it to them.
6. After half of his day was spent at their homes, he would close a small percentage of them.

This sounds just like my business, I thought. *I can't even begin to count how many appointments I've had where I spent two or more hours just answering basic retirement and financial questions to get to the point of talking about them, their pain, and how I can help.*

Dave spoke briefly about each of these points, then flipped the slide to show the post-blogging bullet points.

Post-blogging sales cycle for River Pools:

1. Prospects go to Google or YouTube and start doing research on pools.
2. They keep coming across the River Pools blog that seems to answer all of their questions.
3. They opt in on the website to keep getting more free information. Now they are engaged in permission-based marketing, where the prospect is reaching out to the company and granting permission to keep contacting them.
4. Because they were so thorough and had all of their answers, many prospects actually read at least 30 pages of the company's information before calling them to get an in-home appointment.
5. One of the owners would show up to the appointment and, upon arriving at the house, would find an informed and already-sold potential pool buyer. As they engaged in self-serve information before ever speaking to River Pools, a massive shift in consumer behavior occurred.
6. The length of the sales appointment decreased exponentially, and they found 80 percent of prospects purchased a new pool if they read 30 or more pages.
7. And these prospects weren't just self-educating; they were self-qualifying as well.

Wow, I would give anything to have clients prequalifying and pre-educating themselves before they call me up and ask for an appointment. It just seems so foreign compared to how we do things in our industry, though.

"Pretty powerful stuff, huh?" said Dave. "How many of you would like to have a similar prospecting funnel?

"Keep in mind, they were able to stop sending out direct mail pieces every month as well, so their marketing costs dropped drastically, while their income went up exponentially.

"What Marcus has done here is essentially flipped prospecting and marketing on their heads. Instead of interrupting people by sending direct mail and trying to get his foot in the door for an appointment, he now has people seeking him, and even calling him asking for an appointment when they are ready.

"People, this is the core of content-based, permission marketing, also known as authority marketing.

"Let me give you some actual numbers from Marcus's company, so you can grasp just how much of a game changer this was for his business.

"In 2007, when the economy was still doing well, River Pools spent $250,000 in interruption advertising to generate approximately $4 million in total pool sales. Not bad by any stretch of the imagination. But keep in mind, just a year later the owners realized how little control they had of their marketing and sales funnels when their business dried up overnight.

"Yet, in 2011, when the economy was still a mess and luxury spending, like buying pools, was significantly lower than compared to 2007, River Pools spent $20,000 in total marketing costs and generated $4.5 million in total sales. What changed, you ask?

"Well, they went from a swimming pool building company to a company that markets and educates people on pools. And they exploded in profits because of it. Not to mention, their clients and prospects liked and trusted them even more, since they didn't feel like they were being sold to anymore. They were simply being walked down a path by an authoritative expert who they discovered and researched on their own.

"My favorite quote from Marcus was when he said, 'We simply answered our prospects' questions in a candid manner and let truth and transparency change everything.' Powerful stuff! Furthermore, Marcus said the mantra and company elevator pitch at the office went from, 'We build in-ground fiberglass swimming pools,' to 'We are the best teachers in the world on the subject of fiberglass swimming pools, and we happen to build them as well.'

"Which company would you want to build your pool?" Dave asked. "Can each of you see how powerful this could be in your own practice?"

Everyone nodded. Personally, I was blown away by what I had heard so far today. I couldn't believe how simple this was, yet hardly anyone in our industry had ever thought to do it.

I thought, *We all keep our knowledge so close to our hearts, as we don't want to give anything away until people come and meet with us.* I assumed that if I gave too much of my knowledge away, most consumers would just go do it themselves.

But I could see how it would have just the opposite effect—where consumers would be driven to you as the authority. I was getting really pumped to head home and share all of this with Jen, and even Judy.

Speaking of Jen, let me see if she tried to call or text back.

I looked down at my phone, and there wasn't a single message or missed call from her. *Gosh, I hope something isn't wrong. But more likely than not, she is trying to get back at me for forgetting to call her my first night here.*

I had been married to Jen for many years, and I knew exactly how she reacted to situations when she was hurt or angry. *I will have to do something nice for her when I get back. Perhaps take her on a surprise date to celebrate my newfound authority marketing knowledge. She could probably even help me come up with common financial questions to answer on my new blog.*

17

WEBSITES FOR DUMMIES

"So, we have one more slide left, and then I will let you go back outside to get your free drinks and waste away your children's college money and inheritance," Dave said, and we all laughed.

The next slide that appeared was a picture of Superman, but instead of a big "S" on his chest, someone had photoshopped in a big "A." And then there was big, bold text across the bottom that said "Authority Advisor."

I wrote down on my notepad, *Goal at Kennedy Financial: Become an Authority Advisor.*

Dave started up again. "Can anyone tell me the #1 reason to have a website? And this applies not just to financial advisors, but any small business or independent businessman or business-woman. Any guesses?"

"For credibility," blurted out an advisor near me.

"Wrong!" Dave yelled back. "Who else has a guess?"

"To create content so you can become an authority marketer," I called out.

"Someone get this guy a napkin to wipe the brown poo off of his nose," Dave said. The entire room burst out laughing, including me.

Dave then said, "Actually, that is a true statement, and it is clear you have been paying attention today. However, that is not the #1 big-picture reason to have a website in this day and age. Any other guesses?"

"To generate leads," said another advisor close to the front.

"Getting close, but that still isn't the #1 reason to own a website today," replied Dave. "Any other guesses?"

The room appeared to be all out of guesses, as it went silent.

"Let me enlighten you," Dave said. "The top reason to have a website is to *make money.*" He then became quiet to let it sink in.

"And not just sporadic, cross-my-fingers-and-hope-something-is-coming-in money. I am talking about money that you can track and depend on, money that is consistent from your website.

"Now this doesn't mean that you have to sell something like financial plans or T-shirts from your website. Although all companies are the same in terms of needing a website to make money, they all make money in different ways.

"For instance, our friend Marcus of River Pools could precisely track on the site how much the company had to spend in terms of time, hosting, and even some native advertisements. He could also track exactly how many clients the company closed from website contact. That is called making money from a site, folks.

"For most of you in this room, making money equates to leads generated from your website that convert into clients. After a while, you will have metrics. For instance, if you know that for every 200 website visitors, you can convert 10 percent into leads, then you know you will have 20 new people in your funnel.

"And then, if out of those 20 new leads, you find out that you can convert two of them into new clients like clockwork, then that is making money. And just like farmers who can scale their crops, once you have metrics like this, you can start scaling your content and even some permission marketing native advertising and grow it until you can't handle anymore.

"The magic of this authority content marketing is that it is scalable. And it can be like having a money tree in your backyard if you do it correctly.

"For instance, let's say that you know the following stats:

- Your average client has $400,000 in assets with you.
- You charge 1 percent to manage your clients' money, on average.
- For every 200 website visitors, you convert two of them into clients.
- So for every 200 visitors, you bring $800,000 of new assets to your practice.
- The lifetime value of each of these two clients is $80,000 (I get that by assuming you keep your clients an average of 10 years at the 1 percent managed money spread).
- That means you need to do everything possible to either create content or spend money to drive people to your site, as long as the acquisition cost is well under $40,000 per client. Of course, if it even takes you 10 percent of that, then something is wrong.

- Think about if you could get 1,000 new unique visitors per month. That means it would generate 10 new clients every month. And if your average client has $400,000 in assets, that is approximately $4 million per month that you would be bringing in from your website!
- Now, of course this number saturates at some point, but you keep fueling the fire, and you stay on top of the metrics until you break even. And then you let your organic, free content marketing continue to bring in new clients while you nurture your crazy fast-growing book of business.
- People, this is how some of the super-successful Internet marketers are doing it. And trust me, this is the ultimate authority and control of your sales funnel.

Dave continued, "OK, so can everyone understand that your only goal and your only objective with your website is for it to make you money?"

Everyone nodded.

"Great, now let's talk a little bit about how you can best turn your website from a credibility-only, static, boring piece of Internet rubbish to a lead-generating, money-making machine.

"To begin, it all starts with content. And not just any content, but valuable content, like our friend Marcus showed us answering top questions people had about pools.

"For you seminar producers in the crowd, the easiest thing you can do is have a professional videographer record your seminar and then put it on your website, where you could be giving your seminar 24 hours per day. Not to mention, you're attracting people like me who are too busy to want to spend an evening eating your free dinner to find out if you have anything special to offer.

"And if you can't afford a professional videographer, you can simply take any PowerPoint presentation and record it on your computer using a screen-capturing software like Camtasia. The bad news is that they won't see you in action, but they will hear your voice and see your entire presentation. And this ranges in cost from free to under $100, depending on what software you choose.

"This is how you can educate, build trust, build authority, and let prospects learn about your services from the comfort of their homes. Not to mention, you don't have to feed these people.

"Now, for those of you who raised your hands about being on the radio, you have a huge advantage here on the web. Assuming you, your compliance team, or your radio station has been keeping the recordings of past shows, that is a boatload of incredible content that you could be using on your site.

"The easiest thing would be to just upload the .mp4 files on your site and have it be like a podcast where prospects can listen to you any time of the day. The next step would be to use a service like www.rev.com to transcribe all of your past shows and put them into text. This could result in hundreds of blogs and even PDF handouts that you can use to become an authority in no time at all. Don't ever be afraid to reuse old content that you did offline, and don't ever be afraid to use the same content in multiple fashions, such as converting audio or video into text.

"But really, the main point of all of this is to start sharing your unique, powerful message on the biggest platform in the world. If you truly believe that you can help people and that you have a powerful message to share, then you are actually doing both yourself and your ideal clients a disservice by not sharing it online. Stop being afraid of the Internet and embrace it. It can change your life, just like it did for Marcus and countless others in all kinds of industries.

"There is simply no other medium that can leverage your time, your authority, and your *income* like the Internet. And just like the super-successful farmer who learns how to scale and leverage his or her time, you will learn how using the Internet to sell for you not only creates more income, but also creates more freedom and time for you to do other things you enjoy. I am talking about a complete *lifestyle* change here, folks.

"Moreover, this simple action of sharing your thoughts and message is how big names in your industry like Suze Orman, Dave Ramsey, and Jim Kramer, were initially found and, over time, became household names with tons of authority. And the worst-case scenario is that you have tons of great content out there and never lose a client again due to lack of authority or presence online."

Ouch, I thought. That comment stung.

Dave continued, "Let's do a quick live example before we wrap this thing up. Pretend that I am ticked off at my financial advisor, and I am finally ready to make a move. My advisor is a well-known advisor in Los Angeles and works with some other top seven-figure earners. If I do make a move, it will have to be to another expert and financial authority who works with high-net-worth individuals like me.

"So who in this room wants to take a stab at earning my business based on what I can find of you and your business online? I will pick someone if I don't get a volunteer," Dave yelled out.

I really pray that he does not pick me. My web presence is so embarrassing. Finally, a guy a few rows in front of me raised his hand.

"Thank you for volunteering, sir. What is your name?" asked Dave.

"Bill Hamilton," the advisor called out so the room could hear.

"Great," said Dave. "And Bill, tell me the name of your firm."

"I own my own RIA; it's called Hamilton Financial Advisory Services," he said.

"Excellent. So, Bill, what I am going to do in front of the entire room is get on Google and see what I can find about you. I am going to do this just like prospects would after they meet you.

"Imagine that we just met for a couple of hours, I like you so far, and now I am going home to do some research on you before I move my millions of dollars from my old advisor to you. Let's see if you pass the test."

"Is it too late to change my mind on this?" Bill asked with a laugh.

"No, sir. You are stuck," said Dave. "So the first thing I am going to do is Google your name, Bill."

He typed "Bill Hamilton" into Google on the screen for all of us to see.

"Let's see what we have here," Dave said. "A couple of LinkedIn profiles, a couple of Wikipedia entries about Bill Hamilton the biologist and Bill Hamilton the politician. Even a Bill Hamilton who builds surfboards. But none of these on the entire first page of Google are you, Bill. And we all know that very few people make it past the first page of Google. Bill, is this correct that none of these people on the first page are you?"

"Yes, that is correct," Bill said in an embarrassed tone. "I guess it is one downside of having a somewhat common name."

"Well, don't worry yet, I am not finished," said Dave. "Let me now search for Bill Hamilton financial, as that is what I would do as a consumer. Let's all look up here on the big screen to see what I find.

"OK, well the first page is a Bill Hamilton from UBS, and then we have another Bill Hamilton who works for Raymond James. Are either of these you?" Dave asked.

Bill looked incredibly embarrassed now and meekly said, "No."

"Hmmm. Well, this fourth entry looks promising. It's a LinkedIn profile. Let me click on it. Is this you, Bill? It sure looks like you from the picture."

"Yes, sir. That is my LinkedIn profile," Bill said.

"OK. Well, honestly, it is not bad, but it also isn't good either. Keep in mind my current financial advisor is published in all kinds of magazines, trade journals, and has even been a featured speaker on CNBC. So when I go to decide if I am going to make a switch to you, can you see how not having a web presence or any third-party credibility could kill the entire deal?"

Bill answered, "Yes, sir."

Dave continued, "Because quite honestly, if I am going to invest my hard-earned money with someone, he better be the best damn expert in the country. And Bill, experts have website presence because we have been trained to subconsciously believe that if you are an expert, then you must be found online.

"Can anyone name one expert in the country who is at the top of his or her game and isn't all over the Internet with countless examples of authority?" Dave asked.

"Of course not!" he answered his own question. "And even though they are all ordinary people just like you and me, celebrities, athletes, and experts have conditioned us to believe that if you are anyone or anything special, you better be able to prove it online."

"Now I realize that some of you might go back to the old saying, 'But my business is different. My clients are older and not on the Internet as much.'

"All I can say to that is, keep telling yourself that as you watch your company go extinct if you refuse to adapt. I have yet to find an industry or a small business that is immune to this trend of being online as an expert. And if you don't consider yourself an expert at what you do, then get out of the business and go get a corporate job where you can blend in and be safe.

"I'm sorry for the tough love, but the financial services industry needs to hear this more than almost anyone. Your industry's late arrival and late adaptation to pretty much everything is costing many of you lots of money," Dave said by way of concluding his passionate pep talk.

That was a pretty painful reminder of why I lost the Smiths. I couldn't help but wonder if I would have been able to save them had I been all over the web and looked like the authority they were searching for.

At the time they explained their reason to me, I thought they were crazy. But after hearing Dave speak, I felt like I understood where they were coming from; and quite honestly, I probably would have had second thoughts myself had the roles been reversed.

Bonus Slide

"OK, for many of you, all of this probably makes sense, but it is like drinking out of a fire hose. I am willing to bet that most of you will get home from this conference all jazzed up to start doing permission-based content marketing to gain authority in your marketplace, but you will have no idea where to start. That is why I created this bonus slide for you. These are the exact same points that I use and give to my top 50 clients who pay me disgusting amounts of money. So, if you are going to take any notes today, take notes on this," Dave said.

He clicked his slide changer, and up popped a bunch of bullet points with the title *The Steps to Website Mastery and Authority.*

- Know thy ideal customer. Become an expert or a specialist to a certain niche. Riches are made in niches.
- Tell your visitors who you are, who you help, and why. Remember the formula, "I help ________ do/create/build ________, so that they may _____________."
- Have an incredibly clear call to action on your site. If 100 people visit your site, all of them should be able to immediately tell you exactly what the #1 action is that you want them to do on your site.
- The call to action needs to stop your ideal visitor in his or her tracks. It needs to be useful and something that will solve a key problem that your ideal client is having.
- Always ask for a visitor's name and email at a minimum in return for you giving them the valuable free widget.
- Keep your site clean and simple. Less is more when it comes to websites as a confused visitor is a gone visitor.

- Use PAS (Problem, Agitate, Solve) throughout your site and blog.
- Answer your ideal customers' questions.
- Always add value.
- Track everything.
- If your website isn't making money after nine months of consistent content and testing, then something is wrong.
- Keep testing everything.
- Get an auto-responder and drip emails on your leads once per week.
- Add a new piece of content (either blog or video) once per week.
    - Focus on ranking in Google for low competition, high-converting keywords and keyword phrases.
    - Write content that your ideal customers like to read, not what you like to read.
- Build your list. He who has the biggest list has the biggest bank account.
- Nurture, communicate, and build rapport and goodwill with your list.
- Never try to build a website yourself. Hire it out to the pros and do what you do best, which is spread your message and then sell through permission marketing.
- Remember that the #1 goal of a website is to make you *money*.

"All right, I am going to end this presentation by not just highly recommending, but begging you to buy the following two books if any of this authority and permission marketing interests you. The first book is Seth Godin's *Permission Marketing*, and the second one is Jay Baer's *Youtility*.

"And remember, this isn't just about authority. It is also about changing your lifestyle. It is about working smarter and multiplying yourself and your sales message on the largest platform in the world.

"When done correctly, it would be like magically having exact replicas of yourself out there selling for you 24/7.

"Well, my time is up. You all have been a great audience to speak to. Thank you for participating, and I wish you all the best in your future endeavors as financial advisor authorities," Dave said as he walked off the stage.

18

TIME FOR CHANGE

The entire flight home, I couldn't stop thinking about Dave Utley's talk with us. In fact, I was just about to go through my notes a second time, as I was determined to get home and actually implement his ideas to become an authority advisor.

This had to be the marketing platform I was looking for, and I couldn't imagine anything that would give me full control of my sales pipeline like permission-based content marketing. Not to mention, I would never lose a potential client again for not being found online.

The other thing on my mind was Jen and the kids. I still had not been able to reach her, and she had not attempted to contact me a single time since my first evening in Vegas. She had tried to prove a point in her stubborn way before, but this was taking it a bit too far. I hoped they were OK.

Home Alone

As I pulled up to the house, I was excited to see my wife but also a bit anxious about how ticked off she was. I hit the garage door opener and immediately noticed that her car was gone.

It was Sunday afternoon, and normally we hung around the house after church. I wondered where she could have gone. I had sent three text messages to let her know what time to expect me, and I knew that she received them, because it showed "Read" on my iPhone texts.

I walked into the kitchen, wondering where my family was, and I came across a note on the counter.

It read:

Steve, I needed some time alone. I took the kids over to my mom's house. Please just give me some space and time to think all of this through.

I still love you.

Jen

I was speechless, and my gut started to wrench like I was going to throw up. I expected Jen to be upset, but not at this level. I pulled out my phone and tried to call her.

No answer. I left a message to let her know I was home, that I had read her letter, and that I really wanted to talk with her.

I couldn't think of anything else, so I called her mother's house.

"Hey, Mrs. Hardy," I said as she picked up the phone. "It's Steve. Is Jen there?"

The other end of the line became quiet.

"Mrs. Hardy, are you still there?" I asked.

"Steve, she is here but says that she isn't ready to speak to you yet. She said please don't come by either. She will call you in the next 48 hours. This is all that she wants me to relay to you. I'm sorry, Steve, but I have to go now," her mom said as she hung up the phone.

Great, I thought. *I came home excited about a new transformation, and I walked into a war zone.* I could only imagine her mom now hated me after hearing Jen complain and throw me under the bus.

I began to wonder if she had corrupted our children into thinking I was a bad father, too. Hopefully she had the courtesy to keep them out of this.

I woke up on the couch in a sleepy daze and looked up to see that the TV was still on. The TV clock told me that it was 6:05, but I was so out of it, I didn't know if it was morning or night.

After I got my bearings, I realized that it was the morning already. I had fallen asleep on the couch after trying to watch TV to get my mind off Jen leaving me, and I must have been so tired that I slept through the entire night. I probably needed it.

Well, now that I was up, I figure I might as well hit the office, get Judy up to speed on the new plans, and start implementing them to get my mind off of Jen and the kids until I heard from her. It was going to be tough to not think about it.

At the Office

"So, let me get this straight. You think by blogging and answering consumer questions, we can create new leads?" asked a skeptical Judy. "If it were that easy, why doesn't every advisor do this?"

"I never said that it was going to be easy, Judy. It could take many months for this to work, which is why most advisors never do it. They just don't have the patience, as we all want prospects *today.*

"I have been like this as well, as I would rather pay for leads or prospects today instead of building an organic, long-term lead funnel. Most of us just can't seem to think long term with regard to marketing and prospecting, and if it isn't instantaneous, we seem to think it won't work," I explained.

"But Steve, is it really smart to be giving out all of your best advice on a public forum? Are you not worried about our competitors stealing your advice and ideas? Or, just as bad, if you give our ideal prospects too much information and answer all of their questions, why would they need us for advice?" Judy asked.

"Great questions, Judy," I said. "This is all about authority, and authority trumps everything. If a competitor took my ideas or information, at some point they would be exposed as a poser. Think about all of the best experts in the world who openly share their information and advice on the TV, online, and in magazines. Do you think they are worried about people stealing their info? Not a chance. They know that the perceived value of their authority trumps any competitor who might get some free info.

"And with regard to my prospects getting most of my advice and not needing me, that is a risk I am willing to take. What studies have shown is that the majority of people who are doing research love the free education and want to have a big picture idea of how things work, but they don't necessarily want to do it themselves.

"In fact, most of them want to have the best expert implement everything for them. And if I am educating them online, whom do you think they will choose as their advisor? And if someone really does get enough of their questions answered from me to do it all by themselves, talk about some great karma. I could only imagine that they would turn into a big referral resource for me when they are telling friends how they learned so much about personal finance," I explained to Judy.

"Interesting. It kind of makes sense when you explain it that way," said Judy. "But what about building a website, hosting, and this thing that I keep hearing about called SEO? You don't know the first thing about those things."

"I am going to hire it all out. The speaker at the conference gave us some great resources to hire out for all of it. In fact, we can find experts to do each thing on a site called www.elance.com.

"The only thing I need to do is start sharing my message, my seminar, and my voice with the public on the world's largest stage. The rest of it I will hire out. And we will have something called an autoresponder that will automatically email our list, so you won't have to lift a finger."

"I like the sound of this autoresponder already," Judy said with a laugh.

"All right, I see that I have back to back appointments starting at 11 a.m.," I said. "After they are over, let's order in some lunch and start contacting all of these web gurus to get this entire thing built out and ready for me to blog. There is a course that we can purchase as well that will teach us how to blog, how to optimize the blog to be found in the search engines for our desired key-words, and how to supercharge the content being found."

"Sounds good, Steve. This should be a fun experience. And if it really does work like you say it does, it certainly will change your business forever," Judy said.

Family Feud

Judy and I spent the entire afternoon getting everything in place to start this permission-based content marketing platform. I wondered how many other advisors from the Dave Utley conference came home and took action like I did? I was pretty proud of how much we did the first day back.

But now I was home, and all I could really think about were Jen and the kids. I had the phone in my right hand, and I wouldn't let it out of my sight, as I didn't want to miss her call.

As I sat alone eating a Chick-fil-A sandwich and fries, I heard the sound of the garage door opening. I put down my food and rushed over to the garage to see if it was Jen. As I opened the kitchen door that led out to the garage, I could see the front of Jen's BMW pulling in.

"Hey there," I said to Jen, for the first time in many years not knowing exactly what to say to my own wife.

"Hey, Steve," she said.

It appeared as though she had been crying on the way here as her eyes were a bit swollen, and her makeup was smudged under her eyes.

After some uncomfortable silence, I took the lead and said, "Jen, I am really sorry for everything. Not just for the missed call in Vegas, but for the past few years of not being the best husband and father. I was so concerned with growing my business that I let it run me. I kept justifying everything by saying I was doing it to provide for you and the kids, but I can now see that I was wrong."

Jen interrupted, "Steve, it isn't just the past few years. It has been like this ever since you started your own company. You kept telling the kids and me that it would just be one more year. To just wait it out one more year, and then you would be at the top of your game, that your practice would be running more on autopilot, and that all the hard work, long hours, and neglect would pay off for our family.

"And Steve, we wanted to believe you, but each year it was the same story. You keep working longer hours, you keep ignoring your wife and family, and you can't even seem to take a full week off without the wheels falling off. And quite honestly, I am not sure I can take it anymore. That is why I decided to finally leave, as I didn't think you would ever take it seriously otherwise."

"Jen, please give me one more shot. I had a huge breakthrough at this conference, and I promise you that it will be different this time. Let's agree on some rules and goals and work on this together… as a family," I begged.

"Steve, this just feels like déjà vu. Why should we believe you this time? What is going to make it different this year? And why can't you just be content with what you have built? Do you really need to be the largest advisor in all of Orlando?"

"Jen, I don't think you totally understand. Even though we have a nice house, nice cars, and live a pretty good life, we have hardly saved anything for retirement. Almost everything is going back into the business, and we spend pretty much anything left over.

"Yes, we have some savings, but it certainly won't get us through retirement. Especially after you figure in our kids' education, weddings, and just life in general with inflation and rising health care costs. And the residual income I have built is great, but it certainly isn't enough."

I continued, "Jen, I have finally realized that I have no control over my business and that it is running me more that I run it. I know absolutely nothing about marketing, and I have been thinking about all of this the wrong way for years.

"But the exciting news is that I really did have a breakthrough at the conference. It won't happen overnight, but it will happen, I am sure of it. In fact, I won't let it fail... and I won't let our marriage fail. For the next six months, the only things that are going to get any of my attention are our marriage, children, and content marketing."

"I hope you are right this time, Steve. We haven't given up on you, but we aren't going to put up with the excuses and neglect any longer. If I continue to see that you are more in love with your business than the kids and me, then I will be forced to go the divorce route.

"I am sorry it has come to this, Steve, but this was your creation. And now it is up to you to fix this and earn our trust and love back. Life is too short to become so affixed with a business that you miss out on your kids growing up and your wife growing distant," she said, as more tears rolled down her face.

"Jen, you have my word that it will be different this time. And if you don't see a big transformation in the next six months, then I won't blame you if you want a divorce. You have my word on that. Now can you bring yourself and the kids back to our house so we can work on becoming a family again?" I begged.

"They are out to dinner with my mom and will probably be back late tonight. I will head back there and we will all sleep at my mother's house tonight, and then let's both take tomorrow afternoon to map out what our ideal marriage looks like. And then the entire family will be back tomorrow evening to see our new and improved husband and father."

"I can't wait," I said, truly meaning it for the first time in years.

19

NEW FAMILY LIFE, NEW MARKETING LIFE

During four weeks, I accomplished so much both personally and in my new marketing venture. I changed my entire schedule to where I left the office every afternoon at 4 o'clock, I was taking my wife out on a date every Friday night, and my kids were seeing so much of me, I think they were finally wanting to not see me so much for the first time in their lives.

Judy and I found a great web developer on www.elance.com who built out our site on a great-looking WordPress theme. We now had a blog ready for content, and we even paid for a videographer to come in to the office and do some professional videos. I tested out the formula of exactly what I do, whom I help, and what problems I help people solve. And it turned out excellently.

I ended up going with what is referred to as a hybrid site, where my blog and my corporate/professional site were blended together. I decided that I wanted one main site where prospects and clients could find me in the search engines and learn everything they wanted to about finance and retirement through my blog, and also learn anything they wanted to about me or my company on the home tab.

The site was very clean looking, and the call-to-action was impossible to miss, not to mention the headline was pretty catchy.

On this particular day, Judy and I were going to sit down and outline the top 100 questions and problems we heard over the last year from our clients and prospects.

We were going through our emails to find old questions; we were going to go through all of the old seminar questionnaires that we kept on file to jot down any and all questions people left; and then we were going through my seminar to create some Q&A from the best slides.

Once we had 100, that would be the basis for the blog, and my goal was to answer two questions per week, so that after a year we would have over 100 blog posts.

One of the content marketing gurus we followed claimed that all of his research had shown that something magical happens in terms of showing up in more and more page one Google searches when a website hits 100 unique pages. So 100 new posts was our big goal for the year.

It was now the end of the afternoon, and Judy and I managed to get 94 great questions that we could answer. We knew that we could find six more over the next week, and my job now was to start where every Internet marketer had to begin... with blog #1.

It was exciting and stressful at the same time. The great news was that I had an entire outline for a full year on what I needed to write about. The bad news was I had no idea how to write well.

In fact, English, grammar, and literature were my most hated and dreaded classes all through high school and college. But I knew that I had to suck it up, and I had read that many of the top bloggers in the country were also bad writers. The secret wasn't actually perfect grammar; it was to speak just as if you were communicating to someone, and I was good at communicating to clients. So, I just had to pretend to speak through my writing.

My other fear was, what if this didn't work? It all made sense when Dave spoke about it, but were there really that many of my ideal clients searching for information on the web?

Deep down, I knew there were. I couldn't think of a single client who didn't get online on a daily basis. In fact, I forced my clients to be on the web to check their account balances and to download any forms.

Not to mention I lost my biggest prospect of my life all due to the Internet, and I knew that everyone seemed to prefer to do research and get education on the web. It certainly beat the old way of either going to the library or having to meet with a salesperson to find out anything.

I thought back to just a year earlier when I purchased my wife's BMW. Although I was a salesman, ironically I hated dealing with other salesmen. And going into a car dealership and dealing with a car salesman was not exactly on my list of fun things to do. So, with this car, I decided to hit the Internet before going in to a dealership. And I was shocked at how much information was out there.

The main BMW site gave me the ability to build the exact car model that we wanted down to the very last detail. I could even pick the kind of speakers we wanted and what color of thread we wanted on the leather seats. It then spit out the MSRP number and an estimated dealership price. I now had some powerful information in my hands, and I was incredibly pleased with how transparent everything was about this car online.

My next searches revealed some great sites that gave reviews of the exact BMW we wanted, and we even found some reviews on the type of wheels that we wanted, which confirmed that we were getting some great wheels for the car.

Then I started hitting all of the BMW dealership websites in the Central Florida area, and most of them had their entire inventory online, including total price. I found two dealerships that actually had the exact car build that we wanted on their lots.

I did some quick math, took a certain percentage off of the MSRP price as the price I was willing to pay, and then made a phone call to the first dealership... dangerously armed with all of the information I needed.

I asked for the sales manager and told him the exact car that I wanted. I informed him that I didn't need to come in and test drive the car, and that I would prefer to not deal with one of his salespeople.

Finally, I told him the price I was willing to pay, and he put me on hold to do some math of his own. He came back two minutes later and said we had a deal. I drove down to the dealership that afternoon, was ushered in directly to the manager's office, and drove away with a brand-new BMW that day with no hassles, haggles, or stress.

At the end of the day, I was an empowered buyer in buying mode, and all parties came out winners. I got the price I was happy with and didn't have to deal with a dreaded car salesperson, and the dealership made money on a car that they didn't have to spend any money on, or any of their salespeople's time on, to get it off the lot.

I was starting to understand how powerful this whole permission-based and transparent marketing was in terms of truly benefiting all parties. No wonder that Marcus guy with the pools did so well.

It was now time to get my first blog posted, and I looked down at my big list and decided that I would knock out the first 10 questions in the next four weeks to build some momentum right off the bat.

I couldn't wait to test out everything that I had been learning with my online content marketing class I purchased from Dave Utley as well. I now knew how to add in tag words, how to target certain long-tailed keyword phrases that my ideal clients would be looking for, and even how to share each blog on all of the social media channels.

I looked down at my first 10 blogs and knew that my ideal clients were looking for this information online:

How to maximize Social Security income
Top 10 ways to save money on taxes
The pros and cons of converting to a Roth IRA
Who should own an annuity?
What are the best ETFs for managed money?
How to compare life insurance policies
Top five questions to ask your financial advisor
The pros and cons of working with a financial advisor
How to create a lifetime income stream
The worst mistakes you can make when doing estate planning

After almost two hours of grueling typing, my first blog was done. It had been years since I had sat down to write 400 or 500 words on anything, and it was tougher than I thought it would be.

However, I actually felt kind of alive and excited that I had created content. There was something rewarding about it, and I was actually pumped about doing another one later in the week.

Now to share it on my social media sites and see whom else I could get to help me promote my first piece of content.

Then, it was a waiting game to see how many people I could reach and add some sort of value to on the web.

20

THE FIRST WEBSITE LEAD

It was then two months since my first blog about maximizing Social Security.

I blasted through my goal of posting my first 10 blog posts within 30 days, and during the second month, I consistently knocked out two each week.

The content coach I was using gave me some great advice: to pick one day per week as my content day. So I blocked out all of my Fridays from 11 o'clock in the morning to 4 o'clock in the afternoon, and all I did was create and post content.

I had enough time to knock out, post, and optimize two blogs each Friday. And there was no better feeling than to head home Friday at 4 o'clock, knowing that I had added some incredible value and created something.

I had forgotten how good it felt to actually create something. I was feeling more alive in my life, and my entire family could sense that something had changed inside of me.

My children were now asking me to come to their sporting events instead of their mom, and Jen couldn't be happier about it.

Jen and I continued to do some kind of date night every Friday evening. Sometimes it was going out to dinner, sometimes a movie, and many times it was just staying in with a bottle of wine and playing board games or watching TV.

Although I hadn't seen any real results from my blogging, I was happier in my personal and business life than I had ever been. It was tough to explain, but I felt like I had a new beginning, that I was finally starting to be in control, even though the results weren't there yet.

I was checking my email every morning, just hoping for a lead to come in. I had my auto-responder with Aweber set up to copy me on any new leads. I had a few leads come in, but they were all existing clients and a few friends and family members.

My site was looking great, and I had the web developer we found on elance.com put in a really attractive floating opt-in box on the top right hand side of my site called "The Seven Must-Know Facts for a Worry-Free Retirement." Because it floated, the headline and call-to-action was always up at the top right of every single page on my site. So if traffic came, the leads were destined to come in.

I had been tracking the website analytics through my free Google analytics account and could see that some slight traffic was finally finding my site.

And it was really incredible to see exactly what people were searching for to find my site. I still couldn't believe how much information and power Google gave the website owner.

I was about to start my 2 o'clock appointment, which was my last one of the day. It was with some clients who had already moved all of their money over to me a couple of years earlier.

It was their annual review with me, and as we began to review all of their different investments and how each one had performed in the last 12 months, Judy came crashing through the door with a huge smile on her face.

"Steve... Mr. and Mrs. Henley, I am so sorry to interrupt," Judy said.

"Is everything OK?" I asked Judy as I bolted from my chair, thinking the building was on fire.

"Steve, I just couldn't hold this in any longer... your first lead came in from the website. It's working, Steve!" she exclaimed.

I didn't know whether to high-five Judy with excitement, or play it off and act irritated with her interruption in front of my clients, so I played it cool and simply said, "Thanks, Judy. That is great news."

The entire rest of the meeting with the Henleys, all I could think about was the lead. It was the first proof of success, and I knew that I would remember this first lead no matter how many leads I ended up producing from content marketing on the web.

Crazy as it sounds, this was one of the best feelings of my career, even though I hadn't made a stinking penny from it yet.

As I said goodbye to the Henleys, I shut the door and then turned to Judy with a big smile and said, "I can't believe it is actually starting to work. Did the lead give us any feedback or ask us to call?"

"Nope, just the lead's name and email. But boy, is this cool. I checked the autoresponder, and it definitely sent out the e-report. Now let's hope the lead reads it and reaches out to us," replied Judy.

The content marketing guru we hired instructed us to build a list and a following as quickly as we could. He said that asking for just a prospect's name and email is really all you want to do.

It will increase your actual leads by a large margin, and it really is one of the keys to permission and trust-based marketing. If you ask for their number and call them immediately after they opt in, you might get a few to book an appointment, but most people will be turned off because they aren't in buying mode yet.

They are in research mode, and this is your chance to be the one to educate them and be there with open arms when they hit buying mode.

"Judy, this is really exciting news. I am off to go celebrate with Jen and the kids. Take the rest of the afternoon off, and let's keep piling on the content throughout this month."

The Lead Tsunami

I was now about to celebrate my six-month anniversary of both my first blog and my new makeover as a family man.

My family life was blossoming, and sadly, I had learned more about my wife and kids in the past six months than I had in the previous 10 years.

But it was a blessing to be able to cut out at 4 o'clock every afternoon and give them the attention that they wanted and needed. Ironically, I realized how much I needed the love and support as well. I had been so caught up in the rat race of growing my practice that I had lost touch with my best support team and cheerleaders.

And even though I was working fewer hours, I was actually on pace to have my best 12-month period since the inception of Kennedy Financial. Funny how things work when you have some balance and are enjoying yourself more.

On the blogging front, once I hit 35 total posts, which happened at the beginning of month five (I couldn't let off the brakes in terms of blogging), something magical happened. I had heard some other Internet marketers talk about the special moment when "the dam breaks," or "the traffic tsunami hits," but I always believed it was just a fable, since I couldn't seem to get much traction except for a lead here and there.

But once I hit the 35-post mark, my traffic spiked and hadn't gone down since. I could only guess it was because I had so many different keyword phrases I was starting to rank for. Not to mention, Google was now looking at my site as a legitimate website, because I was putting out so much unique, readable content each week.

I knew it was readable because viewers' average time on my site kept creeping up every single week.

The best news was that with the large surge in traffic, I had accrued 37 total leads from my website so far. And most of that had happened in the last few weeks, so I had some big momentum going for me.

The bad news was that although I was super excited to see this working, my #1 goal of making money from my site was still not happening. Not a single one of these 37 leads called me or emailed about meeting, but I was not anywhere close to throwing in the towel.

I knew that if I kept sending them great information, answering their questions, and dripping email on them once per week, this would pay off.

So, my entire marketing plan consisted of posting two new blog posts per week and then emailing the better of the two posts out to my list every Tuesday.

This enabled me to get my message out to the entire web, and with one click of a button, 37 people who now knew me from opting in on my site were also exposed to my message.

The goal every week with my email blast was to get them all back to my site where I had a powerful call-to-action on every single page now. If I got them to my site, I knew that chances were pretty good that they would take the desired action.

21

THE FISH AND THE WHALE

Then, I marked the eight-month anniversary of my new and improved life after coming back from Vegas. My wife and I were closer than we had been since we took our vows two decades earlier, and my two children, Ashley and Steven Jr., were coming to me for help on everything from homework to relationship questions. It had really been a complete family transformation.

On the business side, I was still churning out content every Friday, and I felt as alive as an artist must feel whenever he or she finishes a painting.

I broke through the 100-leads mark from my website, and traffic was breaking new records for me each month. It was really starting to get fun.

Judy fielded one phone call from someone who came across my site but just wasn't a fit for us as a client because he didn't have enough money, and a handful of people emailed me with more questions.

In all honesty, I was a bit frustrated that there were no actual appointments on the books yet from this permission-based marketing. I went in knowing it could take up to a year to see legitimate results, but I was starting to lose my patience.

It was Tuesday, and I had a pretty light day in terms of appointments. I came in, said hi to Judy, and then started returning emails like I did every morning when I came in.

As I was going through the last of my emails, I saw one from a name I didn't recognize: Ken Fitzpatrick. The subject said, "Been enjoying your site," and I wondered what this was about.

I opened the email to read:

Hey Steve,

My wife and I came across your site when we were doing some research on annuities. That led us to your blog, where we downloaded your free e-book, which we really enjoyed. We have continued to follow your weekly blogs, and we feel like we almost kind of know and trust you already.

We were hoping to get some time with you to look over our retirement plan, as we know that we have some holes in it, and we want to work with someone like you who is clearly an expert.

Please let me know how my wife and I can get on your calendar.

Sincerely,

Jim and Misty Fitzpatrick

"Judy, did you see this?" I screamed at the top of my lungs. "It is finally working! We have our first legit person raising his hand!"

Judy came bursting in, read the email, and almost burst into tears of joy. For the first time since I hired her, I was hugging my 60-year-old assistant over the excitement of a prospect.

The Fitzpatrick Family

The Fitzpatricks came in the week after I received their email, and we had a great first meeting.

The Fitzpatricks were both 64 years old, still both working, and they brought in a combined $265,000 per year of income. However, they had done a somewhat poor job of saving, considering their income and the fact that they had no children. Combined with the fact that they wanted to continue to spend six figures a year on travel, their two beagles, eating out, and enjoying retirement to the fullest, they actually had a long way to go before they could retire comfortably.

They had amassed a little over half a million dollars of total retirement savings, and after three meetings, they moved every last penny over to me to manage it.

I must say that it was the easiest close in the world, as they came in already closed after reading so much of my content. It really was just like Dave Utley and his buddy Marcus, the pool guy, explained it.

When you have authority, and you empower potential customers with information, you no longer have to sell once they raise their hands. The toughest part is just finding out if you are a fit with them as clients.

The Whale

It was a little over 11 months since I started my new website, blog, and family life.

My relationship with Jen and the kids continued to blossom, and I was at the point where it would be impossible to drag me back into my old routine of letting my business run me.

On the business side, I was still doing seminars, although I had cut the number of seminars I was doing in half.

And the new marketing idea I was about to implement was to send out a direct mail piece similar to the one that I used for my dinner seminars, but it would focus on driving the prospects to a dedicated web page where they could actually watch my seminar from the comfort of their homes.

I would no longer have to pay any money for food or the venue, and the company I was using actually had a guarantee that at least 1 percent of the people would opt in on my site.

So with a 5,000-piece mailer, I was guaranteed at a minimum to have 50 new people give me their information so they could watch my presentation online. Not too shabby.

Of course, I would add all of them to my weekly email drip, and I would also have a pretty powerful call to action at the end for them to book an appointment.

Worst case, I knew based on my tracking that of every 25 people who came into my funnel, one would raise a hand at some point. Not too bad for a cheap postcard mailer. And it helped my website out in terms of overall traffic and time spent on the site, which was excellent in the eyes of Google.

On the Internet lead side of things, I was now up to over 300 total leads, which had resulted in three new clients coming on board, including the Fitzpatricks. I had gotten quite a few more inquiries via email, but most of them were just not a fit.

But the most exciting thing was that I had created these 300 leads without spending a penny in marketing or advertising yet.

All it took for me was setting aside four hours every Friday, and not only was I getting free leads, I was also gaining some nice authority. Someone at the local chamber of commerce found my blog and asked me to speak to his entire chapter about legacy planning. I even got a new client out of it.

A few people at my church mentioned coming across my blog, and even a woman at our local grocery store came up to me and asked if I was Steve Kennedy, the financial blogging guy. I felt like a mini-celebrity.

I was continuing to drip email my new content to my list every single Tuesday, and I was building a pretty loyal following—a tribe, if you will.

I would receive feedback from some of them saying that they enjoyed the blog, or that they learned something from one of my postings, and I always simply thanked them in return. I never went for the close on my reply emails, and I refused to be aggressive.

And you know what? It felt incredible not to have to sell that way anymore. It was one of the most empowering moments in my career when I didn't have to be a pushy salesman. And I could tell my online followers loved it as I continued to hear feedback and even generate some referral followers. The list was growing, and I was beginning to feel the energy building.

In fact, the list was building so fast that a couple of weeks earlier, I had finally told Judy to discontinue sending the auto-responder copy of each lead to my personal email, as my inbox was becoming too cluttered with leads. So now Judy was the keeper of the leads.

It was Friday, which meant content day. But that was only after I put some normal work in; I usually tried to see at least one or two clients or prospects in the morning before 11 o'clock.

I walked my first appointment out to her car after our meeting, as she was a much older widow named Ruth who couldn't walk that well.

I always had Judy offer to pick Ruth up and drop her off whenever she had an appointment, but ol' Ruth always stubbornly refused and insisted on driving herself.

Personally, I was glad that I was inside my office and not on the road with old reckless Ruth.

As I walked back into the office, I could see Judy staring at the computer with her mouth wide open.

"Hey, Judy, why are you looking at the computer like it's the first time you've ever seen one?" I asked with a laugh.

She was silent for a couple of seconds as she finished reading whatever she was looking at. Then, she looked up and said, "Steve, get over here and see this. I don't believe it."

I moved behind her chair to read what was on her screen and saw that it was a new website lead. And not only did the prospects fill out the optional note section, they practically wrote a book.

Here is what we saw.

Name: *Tim and Katherine Chandler*

Email: *timchandler@gmail.com*

Note (optional): *Hey Steve, thanks for all of the hard work, time, and energy that you put into your financial blog. My wife and I found you online over two months ago, and we have been reading pretty much everything that you have posted since.*

The reason we were looking for financial information is because I recently sold my business to a large Fortune 500 company, and prior to the big sale, almost all of our assets were tied up in the company. Because of that, we never felt that we needed a financial advisor or broker as we didn't have that much to manage or advise on.

However, a few months back, we were invited to a free financial dinner seminar right here in our backyard of Macon, Georgia. If you don't know anything about Macon, it is Georgia's second-largest city, but it still feels like a small town.

So small, in fact, that we never wanted to have a financial advisor based out of Macon because we were afraid that he or she might slip up and share information about our money, which we have and always will keep as private as we can.

The reason we decided to go to this particular event was that the financial advisor hosting it was actually out of Atlanta, and he puts on these dinner events all over Georgia. He did an exceptional job, we learned quite a bit, and we really liked the guy. We ended up meeting with him for a couple of hours, explained that we just sold our company for over $32 million, that we had some huge tax issues heading our way this year, and that we needed all of the help that we could get.

We met him a second time and even discussed some general ideas on what he recommended we do, as well as certain products, plans, and tax shelters that we should be looking at.

My wife and I took lots of notes, and the first thing we did afterward was head home and start doing our research online.

We found quite a few things about some of the ideas he shared, but we couldn't really find anything about this advisor for some reason. It was almost as if he didn't exist. And quite honestly, that raised some serious red flags for us. What kind of financial advisor who considers himself an expert or a specialist isn't found online? I know that if I ran my business like that, I never would have sold my company for so much money.

At any rate, we kept coming across your name, and we really enjoyed your candid blogs that were both educational and entertaining. It was one of the few sites we found that wasn't trying to push some product or trying to sell yourself or how great you are, unlike some of these advisor sites we saw.

You came across as an authority who didn't have to use the old sales tricks, and that is the kind of financial advisor we want to work with going forward.

Would you be willing to work with someone like us who isn't in Florida?

Looking forward to hearing from you,

Tim and Katherine Chandler
(478) 555-5555

I didn't say a word. In fact, I wasn't sure that I could. So, I sat down the on the couch in the lobby right across from Judy's desk and began to cry.

I was speechless. I was overwhelmed. I finally had control. I finally had authority.

22

FOUR YEARS LATER

"Jen!" I yelled as I ran down the steps of our home into the kitchen. "You won't believe this. I am being asked to be one of the main speakers at the same convention in Vegas where I met Dave Utley. And they are even going to pay me thousands of dollars to do it!" I yelled with excitement.

"Steve, I am so proud of you! What do they want you to talk about?" she asked.

"They want me to talk all about my transformation from a marketing dunce to an Internet authority in just a couple of years. And, of course, they want me to tell the story about closing the $30 million client on the one-year anniversary of coming to this same event where I originally learned everything.

"The coolest news is that the other main speaker is none other than Dave Utley himself. I finally get to meet the guy who changed my life."

"That is so incredible, Steve. You deserve every bit of it," Jen said as she came over to hug me.

I pulled my head back from her bear hug and said, "This time I am taking you with me as my date. I am not going to risk coming home from Vegas and finding out that you are gone when I get back again. So I figured the easiest way is to drag you along with me."

"Does this mean that we can go to a show like Celine Dion or Cirque du Soleil instead of people watching at Margaritaville?" she asked.

"Absolutely, babe. Absolutely."

The Speech

I was sitting in the green room behind the curtains of the main conference room floor, just minutes away from going onstage in front of the entire group of 1,000–plus RIAs out in the crowd.

I could hear the emcee introducing me, and I started to get nervous. I had been speaking in front of thousands online behind my website facade, but I had never spoken in front of a group this large.

I took a deep breath and told myself that I would kick some butt out there. This story needed to be told, as I knew that there were countless financial advisors in that crowd who needed to hear what I went through.

I was certain that many of them were not alive in their practice or their relationships, just like me four short years earlier.

They were calling my name. I walked out onto the stage and saw over 1,000 faces all staring at me.

I began, "Have any of you ever thought you were a successful entrepreneur and small business owner who was in complete control of your business, your relationships, and your lead funnels... only to wake up one day and realize that your entire business and livelihood, perhaps even your marriage, were completely out of control? Perhaps you found that your business was really running you, and not the other way around.

"Well, let me tell you the story of my life over the past five years and how you can learn from it."

23

THE FINAL CLOSE

I hadn't really closed hard or negotiated anything in years. It had been eight years since I started my blog, and since then I had let my website, emails, and content do all of my closing. By the time prospects came in to see me, they were already closed. They trusted me as an authority, and baby boomers from all over the country now knew my name and what I stood for.

A far cry from my old days of interruption marketing and selling like there was no tomorrow.

But today I was going to have to learn how to close and negotiate again, as there was a lot on the line.

It was crazy to think that I had amassed over $400 million in total AUM in just under eight years, all from online permission-based content marketing.

I finally stopped my last financial seminar once I closed that $30 million whale at the end of my first year of blogging, and I certainly didn't miss all of the marketing expenses that I used to spend.

But today was a tough one for me. Not only was I going into the shark tank with my attorney to negotiate the final sale of my company to a large firm, but they also wanted to buy my blog and my website as well.

It was crazy to think that I had an emotional attachment to a marketing and educational tool like a blog, but I guess it can only be compared to an artist having a love affair with his or her best artwork. It just isn't easy to let go of something that is a part of you.

However, the crazy thing was that my blog was responsible for generating the majority of that $400 million, and everyone knew it. So in some respects, the leads and tribe that were being nurtured every month from that blog had ridiculous value.

My list had grown to over 8,000 people and had become an asset with an enormous amount of power. For instance, if a new long-term care policy came out that I really thought was valuable, I could write up a quick blog post or do a three-minute video, send it out to my list of 8,000 consumers with one click of a button, and within an hour I could usually get anywhere from 12 to 20 people raising their hands, asking for me to send them paperwork on it. It was like printing money.

Ironically, this company hoping to buy me out originally found me by hearing about my large list of ideal baby boomer and retiree clients. They knew that if they had a nurtured list of consumers who trusted my content, they could essentially cross-sell any kind of product imaginable to them.

In fact, during the last meeting with this buyer, we had itemized everything out, and the blog was priced out at $2 million, while my list of approximately 8,000 baby boomers and retirees was valued at $3 million. As you can tell, this was a big chunk of the $21 million that this company was offering for my book of business.

That's right, my blog and, just as important, my list had become huge assets.

I wasn't sure what number we would settle on, or even if we would settle today, but I knew that I was walking away with at least $21 million; and if that wasn't authority, then I didn't know what was.

My final words: "If Your Prospects Can't Find You Online, Then You Don't Exist… "

To learn more about Steve Kennedy's transformation, including how he accomplished his digital success, and how you to can "go digital" and become an online authority, check out www.AdvisorInternetMarketing.com today.

ABOUT THE AUTHOR

Joe Simonds is an Internet marketing-loving, beer-loving outdoorsman who has spent the majority of his career helping financial advisors sell more business, improve their marketing, and communicate better with their ideal clients. He and his brother Luke started Advisor Internet Marketing (www.AdvisorInternetMarketing.com) as a resource to help financial advisors be found online, spread their message, and become authorities on a well-known platform known as the World Wide Web.

Unsurprisingly, he also spends much of his time educating baby boomers and retirees about retirement income planning on sites that he founded and still creates content for, such as www.RetirementThinkTank.com, www.AnnuityThinkTank.com, and www.Annuity123.com.

He was recently voted one of the Top 24 Most Creative People in the Insurance Industry by LifeHealth Pro and continues to try to add value to the insurance and retirement industry in any way he can. He also published another book, *Savior Retirement,* which has sold thousands of copies.

Joe graduated at the top of his class at Georgia Tech and still roots for the Yellow Jackets in all sports, even when they aren't any good.

He and his wife Loren have two beautiful little girls, and they love to travel, see new places, and be outdoors any chance they get.

Find him online at www.AdvisorInternetMarketing.com and @joesimonds on Twitter.

35607353R00128

Made in the USA
Charleston, SC
15 November 2014